W9-AMB-457

THE VIOLIN

Translated from the French by Ed Emery
Edited by Sheila Schwartz
Picture Research by Béatrice Petit
Illustrations by Gilles Alkan
Designed by Rampazzo & associés
Layout and typesetting by Daniel Leprince

Flammarion
26 rue Racine
75006 Paris

200 Park Avenue South,
Suite 1406
New York
NY 10003

Original title: *La Légende du Violon* Copyright © Flammarion 1996.

For the English translation:
Copyright © Flammarion 1996. All rights reserved.
No part of this publication may be reproduced in any form or by any means,
electronic, photocopy, information retrieval system, or otherwise,
without written permission from Flammarion.

Library of Congress Catalog Card Number: 96-86015

ISBN: 2-08013-623-2
Numéro d'édition: 1165
Dépôt légal: October 1996

Printed in France

ST. CHARLES PUBLIC LIBRARY DISTRICT
ONE SOUTH SIXTH AVENUE
ST. CHARLES, ILLINOIS 60174

THE VIOLIN

YEHUDI MENUHIN

with the assistance of Catherine Meyer

Flammarion
Paris - New York

3 0053 00403 5930

In the magic of a moonlit, snowy landscape, the body becomes an instrument. The voice of the cello seems to emerge from the very flesh of the man, and the bow makes his very fibers sing. In this magnificent allegory, all is transparency. Everything quivers in the vibration of this voice: the leaves in the sky, the people, and the animals. What is being expressed through this body-instrument are the dreams of the village's inhabitants, expressed with warmth and sensuality despite the freezing cold of the night.
Marc Chagall (1887-1985),
The Cellist, 1939.
London, Hulton Collection.

The image of perfection. This violin is one of the most extraordinary objects ever fashioned. It is an absolute masterpiece; its voice is so pure and powerful that it seems to come from heaven itself. Stradivarius, its genius creator, was here working on the border of the animate and the inanimate: one single caress of the bow and the violin comes to life. The "Soil."

PRELUDE

A taut string is set in motion, the passive air responds and carries the vibrations to a listening ear. That motion carries music. Hearing is the first sense to develop what might be called "distance touch" in a newborn babe, for it is indeed a form of touch which sets the membrane in our eardrum in motion, the same motion, with the same periodicity and structure that is generated by the vibrating string. The newborn baby hears music first, for speech is unintelligible and it is rather the inflexions of texture, the speeds of different pitches which enable the infant to distinguish between the parents' voices. Color, texture, warmth, amplitude of vibration—these convey musically the feelings of pleasure, pain, fear, comfort, and support which the infant needs. Violin strings are based on the vocal chords which are set in motion, each tuned to a different note, each capable of adjustment in length to different pitches and able to communicate these as the instrument does to the listener. For the child, audible vibrations mark the beginning of a meaningful dialogue.

The first sound that a child hears is music, and the first sound it makes is the effort to create music from noise; meaning from meaninglessness. This is precisely the civilizing process. The importance of music lies in its ability to communicate, and all our efforts go into making it as meaningful as possible. Music is the bearer of every conceivable emotion whether delicate, tender or overwhelming and even cruel. There can be no sharing of emotion without the aural, the meaningful communication through sound. Feeling and wanting precede and create thought and speech, and the secondary visual activities of reading and writing. Our present-day civilization has a dangerous tendency to pass over the aural stage with the result that many of our theories are detached from real experiences which might give some value.

Human communication does not take place solely through the medium of words. The voice of the violin is so rich in possibilities that it goes far beyond the exchange of signs characteristic of written language. The violin fulfills the need for companionship as might a doll, but it is a living, vocal companionship dependent on the gifts of the player and the response of the violin. It is also an object which appeals to the other senses of touch and sight. There is no doubt that the violin is one of the most beautiful objects imaginable, and its varnish can be a warm, smooth almost velvety surface. A violinist cannot feel about a violin but that he holds a means to expression which transcends matter and measure.

This book will explore the predecessors of the stringed instrument, the infinite variety of shapes, forms and purposes which embody the principle of the bowed, vibrating string, as well as the people whose lives have been touched by its music. And I hope it will give some impression to the reader, in both words and images, of the feelings which are evoked by the violin.

No matter how many years, how much work and constant practice, the same magic recurs in the action of the bow caressing the strings, in this motion of fingers on the fingerboard. The same voice is summoned up as if in a dream, and your eyes close to receive this inner sound. At that point, what you hear in yourself harmonizes with the perceptions that come from the outside. Descending into the interior self, you can capture the primeval voice, the purest idea of sound and its color. It has the allure of a prayer, which sweeps the body and the gestures of the violinist along in a surge of devotion. Yehudi Menuhin.

Who can say whether the hunter judges the extent of his range simply by the sound of his bow? The sound of the string stretched to the extreme, when it goes into a higher pitch, perhaps gives the archer a deep sense of satisfaction. It may even be that this music is more important to him than the target bird.
Hunting Scene (detail), Assyria. Paris, Musée du Louvre.

Although she holds an instrument with strings that are plucked, this young woman takes up a position which anticipates that of the first violins, which were placed against the chest. Gracefully and naturally, she lets us share this tranquil moment of listening and expectation, when time seems almost suspended: her delicate *pizzicato* perhaps suggests the expectation of a male voice about to join her in accompaniment.
Figurine from Aegina, Greece. Paris, Musée du Louvre.

THE OBJECT THAT CREATES THE SOUND

Once upon a time, in an age forgotten by time itself, at the dawn of a humanity whose secrets remain a mystery to archeologists, historians, and scholars alike, a taut vibrating string made itself heard—and with this second voice the human being was no longer alone.

Down in the bowels of the earth, deep in subterranean galleries, there are precious archives of humanity's early history. We are on the trail of the first violin, perhaps about to witness the first attempt to tame vibration. On the walls of the Grotto of the Trois Frères in Ariège, a primitive hand has drawn a man disguised as an animal. This character, half-man and half-beast, holds before his face an object resembling a small bow: a convex piece of curved wood which a taut thong holds in shape. The picture dates from nearly 15,000 years ago.

GENESIS OF THE VIOLIN: THE BOW AND ARROW

*I*t was in fact about this time that the bow was invented, enabling man to hunt new quarry in larger numbers and with more certain results. This picture from the Grotto of the Trois Frères raises many questions. The picture shows no arrow—just this crude bow, astonishing in its bareness of detail. Furthermore, we see that the man holds not the wooden bow but the string in front of his face. This might suggest that what is absorbing his attention is the vibration of the string—the sound that it is producing, the

*W*ho is this man dressed in animal skins—is he a hunter or is he a musician? Where is the arrow for his bow? Is he going to kill reindeer and bison, or charm them by making the vibrations of the bow string resonate in his mouth? Is he, before our astonished gaze, in the process of inventing the first violin? In this image, almost 15,000 years old, can be read the entire history of humankind: the secret links between hunting and music, matter and spirit, animal and man. Thousands of years later, the Greeks imagined the god Pan, half-man and half-animal, living in the same way as this caveman in the midst of flocks of animals and playing music just like him. The Grotto of the Trois Frères (Magdalenian era), Ariège. Opposite: a relief from the abbey at Breuil.

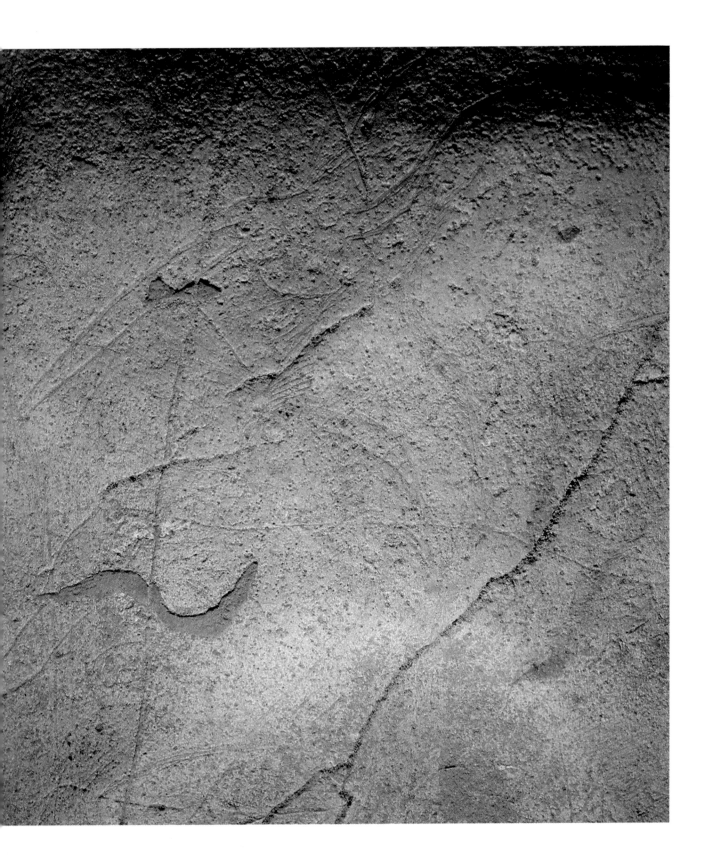

oscillations it is making in the silence—rather than the object that such a bow might launch into space, the absent arrow it could have unleashed.

Could this mean that music came before the arrow, the sound before the deed, that art came before the hunting bow, and that music was so primitively rooted in the depths of humanity as to constitute a need even more basic than that of food? Dreams, after all, do provoke reality. Man would thus have found a

way of creating a vibration, a sound, and only then would he have discovered that this object, as well as being a source of pleasure and enchantment, might also function as a useful weapon.

This form of bow, known today as the "musical" bow, is still found among many African tribes. Sometimes the instrument serves as much to placate the spirits of the forest as to kill animals—a last vestige of the musician–hunter of time immemorial.

*I*n the Seychelles, perhaps thirty years ago, I saw a similar instrument, which came from the Kalahari Desert. It too had the form of a hunting bow, and it had a link, halfway down, between the string and the wood of the bow. This link was movable: sliding it up and down provided either a third or a fifth. I was very struck by this object, at once so pure and elementary, and I felt as if I were seeing something like the first stringed instrument: there, before my very eyes, it was recreating the intriguing myth of the instrument's origins.

I imagine that the first sound ever drawn from a string must have been a *pizzicato*, a plucked note. This is the ancestry of the harp which must have preceded the bowed string by perhaps hundreds of generations. Basically the violin has evolved from this vibration of a string under tension. It is in this balance between the force exercised by the hair of the bow as it pulls the string, and the force exercised by the string as it resists the pull, that the first instrumental musical song is born. It is this very tension that generates the first elements of life.

Sound is thus the product of tension and equilibrium, while noise is the result of chance: rain makes

*T*oday the musical bow is still in use in many African tribes. Here the musician uses his mouth as a resonating chamber: by opening and closing it he increases or decreases the intensity of the sound produced. He sets the string vibrating by means of a wooden stick—not plucked, as one might expect, but made to vibrate with what we might call an ancestor of the bow. This brings us very close to the spirit of the violin, here seen in one of its most pure and primitive forms. The man's expression of attentive listening indicates that he is searching within himself for the colors of the sound he wants to achieve. Musical bow, Upper Volta. Paris, Musée de l'Homme.

a noise falling on the leaves of a tree; a pebble dislodged by a gust of wind makes noise as it rolls on the ground; lightning tearing through the sky makes noise in the form of thunder.

Sound carries within itself the mark of our desire to communicate and to send messages: the spoken word is a sound; the song of the mother as she rocks and soothes her baby is a sound, which must be humanity's very first music. The desire to organize the kingdom of sounds and noises is one of our most powerful instincts: the need to communicate with others takes us back to the most primitive drive of our species.

*W*e cannot, unfortunately, penetrate the mysterious depths of time to study with certainty man's many experiments before he finally hit upon the idea of the bow. We can, however, imagine, intuit, or even dream about the progressive ingenuity of the human spirit.

It is here that we return to the hunt: if the musical bow engendered the hunting bow, the latter, in its turn, inspired the instrumental bow. The hissing of the arrow as it cuts through the silence, the contact of the arrow on the string—such barely perceptible sensations gradually guided the exploration and mastery of the kingdom of gestures and sounds. In a subtle and reciprocal movement between the desire for music and the needs of survival, a new instrument was born. It is no accident that the same word is used both for hunting and for playing the violin: one plays with a bow; one also hunts with a bow. The important element is duration in time, the stretching of sound that enables the instrument to come somewhere close to the human

voice, which is the model it always seeks to imitate. Ultimately, what is created by the string is no longer merely a short, simple vibration in the air—however resonant it may be, as with the harp, the harpsichord, or the guitar—but a continuous line, a sustained and unending melody. The string becomes vocal and the instrument becomes a voice.

Language gives us other evidence of these original sources, since the word "violin" derives from *viole*, which in turn derives from the Provençal verb *viola*. This word is onomatopeic, for it imitates the high-pitched, continuous noise of an object in flight—for example, an arrow that has been fired. The consonant "v" reproduces the hiss of the arrow leaving the string; the diphthong "io" is the prolongation of that noise in space, and the final "la" represents the resolution of this adventure, the conclusion of this small music made by the bow and its arrow.

As for the word "bow" in its musical sense, it also preserves the signs of its origins. *Archet* or *petit arc* in French, *archetto* in Italian, "bow" in English, *Bogen* in German—the languages of the violin-playing world all concur: in each instance the same term is used both for the hunting implement and the musical implement. And in fact, from its beginnings until relatively recently, the violin bow was like a twin image of the hunting bow—one can envision the very first bowed stringed instrument as an encounter between two bows.

*F*rom this distant kinship with the hunting bow, the violin has preserved or rather, has tamed, the stamp of violence: both hunting and music involve an element of violence, and of love, too. The tension of the

string and its struggle against the countervailing forces, the friction or plucking of the string, and the way in which the disturbed equilibrium seeks to return to its former state, the propulsion of the arrow as it cuts through the air—all these quiverings, all these miniature cataclysms also characterize the actions of the violinist. The drawing action of the bow, the friction of the hair of the bow across the string, the transmission of these vibrations to the resonating and amplifying chamber of the violin through the sound post to the back of the violin, all these myriad little earthquakes radiate the voice of violin in all directions.

*T*he sport of archery also bears the stamp of violence. Here the pulling of the bow string requires such strength that the legs have to share the work with the arms. A muscular archer fires an arrow in a careful combination of effort and equilibrium. Engraving by J.-B. Debret, *Cabocle, the Indian Archer*, 1834. Rio de Janeiro, Brazil, National Library.

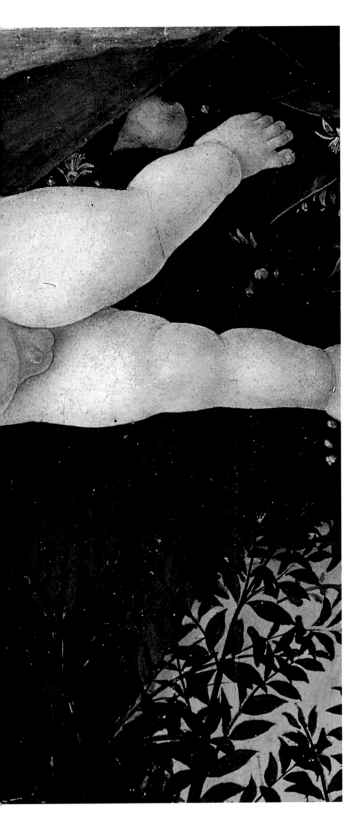

*A*n innocent child, teasing
and blind, Cupid leaves the choice
of his victims to chance.
The delicious wounds inflicted
by Love's archer mark the human
heart as deeply and subtly
as does the violin bow.
Sandro Botticelli (1445–1510),
Primavera (detail of Cupid), 1478.
Florence, Galleria degli Uffizi.

The figure of Cupid, with his bow and arrow, gives us the most beautiful representation of this subtle mixture of violence and love: into his victim's hearts he fires a sharp-edged arrow, the symbol both of wounding and love, of suffering and happiness. Just like the violin, this winged, mischievous child teaches us a lesson of life. In life, each of us passes through cycles of love—including both capture and surrender, demanding and yielding, aggressive and serene. As in yin and yang, as in this profound correlation between the vital breaths that fire our existence, it is essential to keep these two cycles in harmony. We must learn to find an equilibrium between two principles: the bow as mortal arrow, and the bow as giver of melodic breath.

VIBRATION AS AN INNER NECESSITY

*H*ow did humankind arrive at the idea of the bow? Who first thought that it could be used to launch an arrow? Who first realized that the string could be bowed instead of plucked? These slow advances, which take humanity from one stage to another, both intrigue and fascinate me.

We have no way of reconstructing the chain of these ancient discoveries. However, of one thing I am sure—that this progress would not have been possible if the idea of what we are attempting to achieve had not been there from the very beginning. The aim comes first; we are not led there by chance.

Following in the spirit of Icarus, Leonardo da Vinci and many others after him sought long and hard to find the ingenious invention that would enable them to rise up off the ground and into the air. The desire to fly is one of humanity's most ancient dreams, and because this dream is etched so deeply into our being, one day men succeeded in making astonishing machines that were capable of defying the laws of gravity, exploiting the opposition between speed and air resistance by the use of wings.

What happened in the case of flight applies as well to other discoveries, and perhaps also to biology in general. For while it is true that the various animal and vegetable species are led unwittingly onward by the desire to reproduce, as if moved by a huge natural clock, nevertheless, every germinating thing, every

*T*he myth of Icarus evokes one of humanity's most ancient dreams: the dream of flying. But it is also symbolic of the punishment inflicted on those who cannot respect their limits. Against the advice of Daedalus, his father, Icarus flew too close to the sun, which melted the wax in his wings and plunged him into the salty waves. Yet the same spirit of adventure has brought us our greatest discoveries. It is by overstepping the limits imposed by society or reason and listening to the inner voice that both progress and artistic creation are made possible. Stradivari, Guarneri, Mozart, Beethoven, Bartók, and many others are, in a sense, fortunate Icaruses who, for our greater happiness, have allowed themselves to be swept along and overtaken by the genius of their creative power.
Jacob Peter Gowy,
The Fall of Icarus, 1636.
Madrid, Museo del Prado.

*T*he reduction of this human
body to the point of abstraction
is astonishingly evocative
of the anatomy of a violin.
The idol-woman-violin stretches
the pure line of her neck skyward.
All that is needed here
is a male-arrow-bow for
the analogy to be perfect.
Marble idol from Paros.
Athens,
National Archeological Museum.

embryo is also guided by something intangible, by something that escapes us. Each is responding to a secret invitation and justifying an unknown expectation.

In music, as elsewhere, no discovery is fortuitous. Each of the various instruments that has been invented by the human spirit corresponds to a sound image that an individual, a people, or a community carries within it. This image leads them to use the materials provided by their natural environment: thus, in making the violin, men used the trees that grew in their countries (maple and fir in the case of the Italian violin makers); or, if they had no forests, they used cactus, as the Native Americans did, or gourds, or

armadillo skins as in Senegal. The same applies to the horsehair, the silk threads, the lamb or sheep gut, the goatskin, catskin, and snakeskin which, all in their own way, have given form to the inner secret vibrations of each of the peoples concerned.

The world's various musical systems thus derive their *raison d'être* from an inner necessity, a specific resonance. It was not simply by chance, with happenstance as the only guide, that modal music, polyphony, and the tempered scale were perfected by the musicians and composers of the West. Nor was it coincidental that nearly five thousand years ago the Chinese discovered the pentatonic scale. In each case, the process involves a great cross-fertilization between a given environment and a human individual or group. The vibrations mingle with one another, some mixtures creating harmony, others creating dissonance.

Thus, over the centuries, a huge and patient project has been under way, moved by an unconscious determination that has been as pressing as the biological impulse. Only in this way can we understand the enigmatic and prodigious work of the Italian violin makers who achieved that most perfect sound, that miracle of equilibrium and construction which has made the violin the inevitable result of the evolution of bowed stringed instruments.

THE ANATOMY OF EQUILIBRIUM

*T*he shape of the violin is disturbingly evocative of the morphology of the female body. It has no straight lines: everything is curved, shapely, scrolled, and delicate. A voluptuous waist, slender neck, rounded back, each part matches canons of beauty comparable to those of the female esthetic. The English language rightly describes this highly sensual instrument with words that are close to human anatomy: "belly" for the swell of the violin-body which fulfills the violin's basic resonating function, "back" for the backplate, and "neck" and "waist."

The analogy with the human body does not stop here: the varnish of a great violin—a Stradivarius or a Guarnerius—has something of the quality of sun reflected on a silky skin. It has that same warmth, suppleness, I would almost say mellowness, although the only contact I permit myself is to stroke it with the back of my finger. A good varnish has the transparency, the life, and the sparkle of the temperament that vibrates in our hearts.

Finally, the violin is the instrument that comes closest to the sound of a woman's voice. It covers all the soprano and contralto registers and thus reproduces completely that original instrument which we all bear in our memory: the voice of woman, the voice of the mother singing to soothe her child.

*T*he violin has a body, and within the emptiness of that body, within the internal space that separates the belly from the backplate, we find the sound post or, as the French say, the *âme*, or "soul." The sound post is just a small, simple cylindrical wooden post, but it is incredibly important, for it transfers the vibrations from the table or sound board to the back of the violin. The sound post must be strong enough to support the table, since it is subject to tremendous pressure from the strings on the bridge; yet the sound post must be light and supple enough to adapt to the curve

*I*n the diaphanous material of this exquisite dress, two bodies meet: the body of the woman and the body of the violin. The woman becomes violin, the instrument becomes woman. Behind the waisted midpoint of the violin is the waist of the woman. The tailpiece, strings, and fingerboard suggest a human backbone as they reach toward the neck. And the belly of the violin blends imperceptibly with that of the woman. The delicacy, the grace, the curves, the arches, and arabesques of the instrument reproduce, interpret, and magnify the sumptuous model of the female body.
Hermès,
Ready-to-Wear Collection,
Spring–Summer 1996.

*T*he head of a violin is the violin maker's final touch: it is a marvelous way of finishing off an object, because the head, or scroll, both completes and contains the instrument. It thus expresses identity and character. In the violin, as in the human being, the head reveals grandeur, boldness, and generosity. The head of a Stradivarius expresses absolute elegance, without a hint of violence. That of a Guarnerius, on the other hand, evokes horses with flared nostrils, impatient to start a race. The first violin makers surely found the inspiration that guided their hands in the fancies of nature. The tendrils of a grapevine or those of a fern ready to unfold are related to the scroll of a violin and speak as well of the deep relationship between bowed instruments and Mother Nature: they have a similar origin, and the same life animates them.

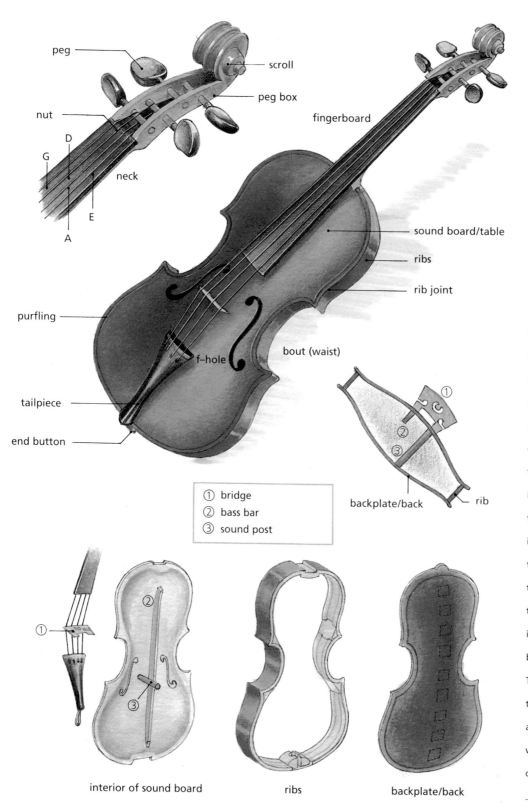

peg

scroll

peg box

nut

fingerboard

D

G

neck

E

A

sound board/table

ribs

rib joint

purfling

f–hole

bout (waist)

tailpiece

end button

backplate/back

rib

① bridge
② bass bar
③ sound post

interior of sound board

ribs

backplate/back

Everyone has seen a violin, but only the violin maker, the one who fashions and assembles the seventy-odd pieces that make up the instrument, knows it from the inside. At its heart sits the sound post, the delicate piece of wood that transmits vibrations from the belly to the backplate, thus making the whole sound box resonate. The tiniest shift in the position of the sound post modifies the entire sound structure of the violin. On the top surface is the sound board or table, the violin's most vulnerable part. An enormous pressure is exerted on the sound board: every time a violin is tuned or the tension of the strings is increased, the bridge holding the strings above the sound board is put to the test. If the bridge falls forward—a result of constant tuning and not checking that the angle of the bridge is correct—the sound board can be seriously damaged. The back of the violin, on the other hand, is more protected and is generally very beautiful— witness the depths of its red or yellow varnishes.

of the table, without blocking its vibrations, and it must also be sufficiently well-fixed not to slip out of its position.

The placing of the sound post is an operation requiring infinite delicacy: the violin maker slips the little wooden post into the violin through the sound hole (one of the f-shaped slots on either side of the strings, also called the f-hole), and positions it at right angles between the table and the back, somewhere below the right foot of the bridge (i.e., on the side where the E-string sits). The exact placement of the sound post is dictated by a mysterious alchemy of sounds: a tiny shift in the position of the sound post can totally transform the sound quality of the violin—for better or for worse. The ideal location will vary from one instrument to another and from one violinist to another. It is here that the instinct and genius of the violin maker come into play.

*A*lthough it is one of the most delicate instruments imaginable, the violin has an animal dimension which is suggestive of its early origins, and again hints at a link between hunting and music. Thus, for centuries violin strings were made from lamb or sheep gut. Gut material offered the perfect balance between the stiffness required for purity of sound and the elasticity on which much of the vibrant timbre depends. Later violin makers came to prefer strings wound with silver, copper, or steel thread, which kept the tuning better. Nowadays we are equally likely to use nylon for the strings.

However, I am attracted to this idea of the violin as a visceral instrument whose sounds, created by the guts of animals, speak the language of the flesh. I like to think of the warmth of the animal penetrating our hearts and bodies.

There is also a further profound link between the violin and the animal: namely, the bow, which is both the violin's accomplice and its mediator. For the part of this implement which bows the strings and produces the vibration is made of a large number of horsehairs. Even today we have not managed to find a more robust, more elastic material. The horsehair is often bleached, although it may sometimes be left in its original colors of black or brown; it comes from Argentina, Canada, or Siberia, countries where horses enjoy wide open spaces and where they have developed a resistance to extremes of climate.

In this way, the violin renders a discreet but constant homage to its Mongol and Gypsy roots. It carries a memory of those peoples among whom man and his horse are one, and where man and violin live together in a form of symbiosis.

*T*he great sensuality of the violin, however, is matched by a tremendous restraint, for the handling of the instrument demands infinite delicacy. Like the flame of a candle that is at once both alive and frail—like life in all its forms—the violin is incredibly fragile, even if this seems astonishing in an instrument capable of such passion and such rich and powerful sounds.

This is why physical contact with the violin should be limited to the fingerboard, on which the fingers are placed, and to the chin rest. The instrument should always be handled with care and respect, and the body of the violin should never be touched. The belly is the instrument's most vibrant, sensitive part; it

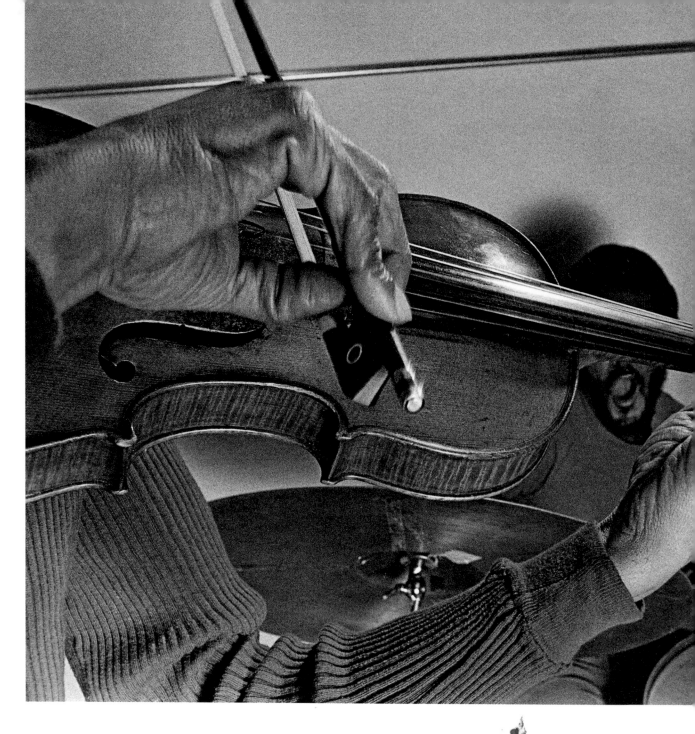

does not respond well to the destructive imprint of fingerprints. As I have already said, the only license I permit myself is to stroke the varnish of the wood with the back of my finger.

When I take my violin from its resting place in the violin case, I take care to hold it only by the neck or, if necessary, by the peg box. If I want my violin to sing, then it will be with the same delicacy and respect that I position it against my body. The violin is a living entity; one should never constrain it, but always leave it free to vibrate.

I am sometimes appalled at the improper way in which some violinists maintain their instruments. One should never allow rosin or dust to accumulate on a violin. The instrument's surface should be kept clean with a very soft silk or cotton cloth.

This photograph shows what is called the "first position" for the left hand (in which the strings are open), and a high position for the right hand (with the bow positioned at the heel, probably because the violinist is about to begin either a powerful attack or a *pianissimo*). In this moment of suspense, one senses that the musician has finished breathing in and that he is beginning, with a gentle exhalation, to make the voice of his violin vibrate. The world represented here is the world of jazz, and behind this gesture one can imagine the tenderness, gentleness, and sensuality of the sound begotten by the instrument's four strings.

One should also clean the fingerboard and the strings every day with pure alcohol or ninety percent eau-de-Cologne; this keeps the vibrations clearer and freer. To dust the inside of the violin, slip a few grains of rice through one of the sound holes, and then shake the grains about inside. When you tip them out, one grain may have a little ball of dust around it. These various forms of care are, in their own way, the mark of the deference that ones owes to this precious and noble instrument.

THE BOW IS TO THE VIOLIN
WHAT THE SWORD IS TO THE KNIGHT

I never cease to be amazed, moved, and full of wonder when I think of the fabulous discovery of the

*A*lmost hidden behind
the instrument, this young person
seems to be drawing rather timid
sounds from the five strings.
This medieval viol is probably
too heavy: despite the delicacy
of the player's grip on the curved
bow, despite the tender cheek-to-
cheek matching of the redness
of hair to the red sides of the viol,
it is alarming to imagine
what kind of sound the unseen
audience must be hearing.
The left hand reveals a fault
characteristic of most student
violinists: the thumb is protruding
excessively over the neck
of the violin. But let us forget
music and allow ourselves
to be seduced by the grace
and finesse of this figure.
Boetius de musica,
fourteenth-century manuscript.
Naples, Biblioteca Nazionale.

bow: only a prodigious spark of genius combined with an incredible inner determination could have inspired the idea that a string could be kept in a state of constant vibration by the continual friction of horsehair.

*T*he first violin bows, as we have already seen, were rather like rudimentary hunting bows. Until the middle of the eighteenth century, they maintained this visual correlation with the hunting weapon to which they are related. I once had the interesting experience of abandoning the modern concave bow, in use since the days of François Tourte, to play with one of these highly convex bows. It was at a recording session of Baroque music. This adventure was a source of new sensations and unexpected reactions. Because the wood of these bows is supple and there is a considerable distance between the hair and the bow stick, there is a slight delay between the initial movement of the bow and the resulting action of the hair on the string: the horsehair reacts a fraction of a second after the movement induced by the wood. This functional characteristic gives a natural accent to the *détaché*: the accentuated notes can be treated as syllables, and are far more marked than with a modern bow, in which you have a simultaneous movement of both hair and stick. Nowadays, in order to obtain the same effect, one would have to apply pressure on the bow stick with the index finger; but the effort required makes it far harder to achieve an accented effect in rapid note sequences with similar naturalness and grace.

Also the distance between the bow stick and the hair characteristic of Baroque bows offers the violinist

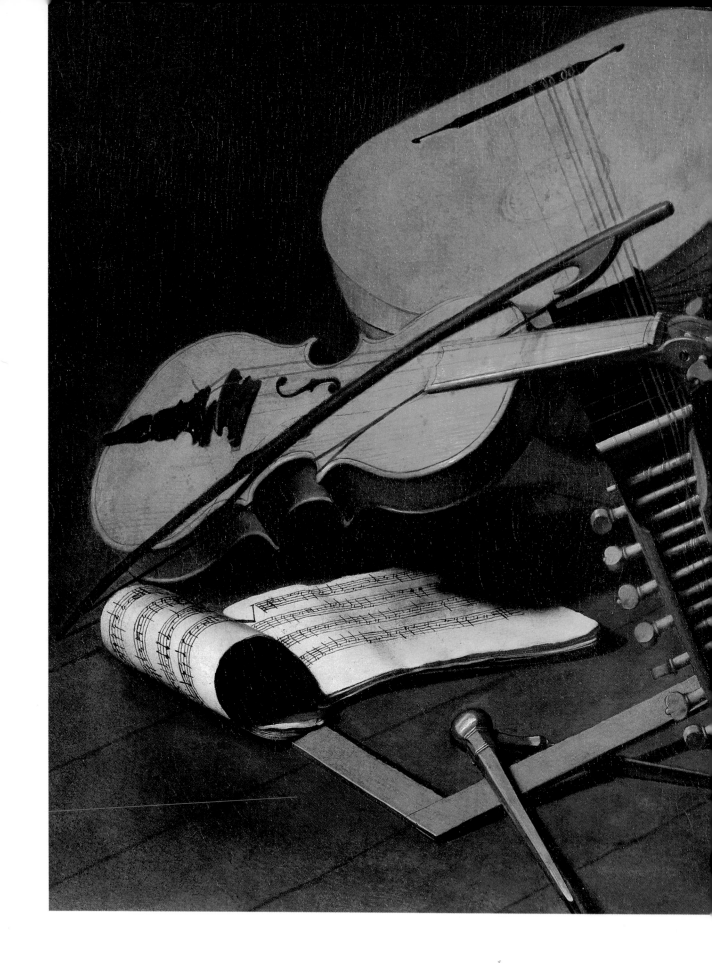

quite naturally an infinite range of nuance, from *piano* to *forte*, and a more subtle modulation of the emotion of the melody.

One final consideration is that the curved bow enables the violinist to deal with more than two strings at once. Its suppleness is such that the same degree of pressure may make all four strings vibrate together.

One has to admit, however, that the modern bow, though it may lack the delicacy of its ancestor, is more powerful and far better suited to styles of playing such as the *spiccato*, or "bouncy" style. It makes the violin a more aggressive instrument in combat. In a sense, it is closer to the sword than to the pen or the feather.

*I*t was in France that the final link in the process of completing the violin was forged. Here, in the latter part of the eighteenth century, the bow as we know it today was created. While the violin, in its most perfect form, was created under Italian skies, in the towns of Cremona and Brescia, the bow owes its subtle alchemy of dimension and equilibrium to the French.

François Tourte (1747–1835) was originally a watchmaker. He came to be known as the Stradivarius of the bow because, like the great violin maker, he devoted his life to the pursuit of perfection, to experimenting with the shapes and materials best suited to serve the art of sound. Eventually, he concluded that the quality of a good bow depended principally on the quality of the wood used in the manufacture of the stick. He therefore chose a Brazilian wood, also known as Pernambuco wood. This was in 1775.

*T*he bow stick portrayed here has a slightly convex profile. As if framed by the bow's graceful proportions, the violin seems ready to launch the rich sounds into the chiaroscuro of the canvas. The score is for an elegant duet with the lute, with its eight plucked strings and neck bristling with pegs. Like many other painters, Caravaggio was attracted by the violin's expressive plasticity and the honey-and-fire sensuality of its colors.
Caravaggio (c. 1571–1610).
Amor Victorious (detail), 1598–99.
Berlin,
Staatliche Museen zu
Berlin–Preussischer Kulturbesitz,
Gemäldegalerie.

Through a process of determined, painstaking work, he perfected the ideal form that came to be known as the Tourte bow; its distinctive features were the concave profile of the bow stick and the slight tapering from the heel, which became more pronounced at the tip. These days his bows are much sought-after and very expensive. My first Tourte was given to me by the violin dealer who provided the first Stradivarius I was given.

Dominique Pecatte (1810–1874) was also a great name in bow making. Unfortunately, he rarely signed his creations, and only experts are capable of recognizing them. Finally, one should not forget Eugène Sartory (1871–1928), an excellent modern bow maker who established a shop in Paris around 1890. He searched for the ideal balance between the weight and length, the resistance and flexibility of the bow. For a violinist, having a good bow is as important as having a good violin. Today France is still the home of many great bow makers, but there have also been remarkable bow makers in many other countries.

*T*he bow is a highly personal object. The violinist gets used to a bow and does not easily change it for another. There is an underlying interplay between this combination of wood and horsehair and the sensitivity and inflections of the violinist.

When I was a child, my father gave me three superb, gold-mounted Sartory bows. The thought of them brings to mind memories of my first trip to Romania. I was eleven years old and traveling to stay with my teacher, Georges Enesco, in his native country.

As soon as I arrived in that legendary land, I succumbed to the enchantment of its dense forests, the

*T*he eighteenth century was the last period for the manufacture of curved bows before the great François Tourte gave the bow the delicately concave shape it still has today. In this picture, the bow stick, barely gripped by the hermit's hand as he lapses into sleep, is splendidly curved. The tip of the stick, where the horsehair joins the wood, is long and tapering. What strange melody could this hermit have been playing, that he was overcome by sleep? Was it inspiration, oracle, or a blessed reconciliation with death that transported him? Joseph Marie Vien (1716–1809), *The Sleeping Hermit.* Paris, Musée du Louvre.

*T*he familiar pre-concert ritual in which the violinist applies rosin to the hair of the bow to give it that sticky roughness that will enable it to rouse the strings to their tremulous action. I have to admit something of an aversion to rosin, and the way it leaves a sticky white powder on the velvety smoothness of one's violin. For the violinist, the bow is crucial: the balance between its weight, length, resistance, and suppleness has to be perfect. Once a violinist becomes accustomed to a bow, it is not easily abandoned, just as a knight would not easily have given up his sword. Yehudi Menuhin, February 1967.

---

nobility of its mountains, the close relationship of its people to nature, and the harmony that ruled among them, whatever their condition. I shall speak later of the secret lesson that country gave me, but first the story of my Sartory bows.

We were staying at Sinaia, a small town that owed its fame to the presence of the king's summer palace a few miles up the mountains. Enesco had his summer residence there—the Villa Luminisch, or "Villa of Light." Autumn had taken possession of nature, and the Carpathians were a blaze of color, fired by a kind of divine painter's madness which threw the colors of the sun on to the leaves of the trees. In Sinaia, there was a small marketplace where peasants came to sell their handiwork, in particular cotton blouses, hand embroidered with great delicacy and wonderful originality. There I met some Gypsies, who were playing music to entertain the people. One of the violinists was very young, and he played with fervor and passion. What I found astonishing was that he was able to get such wonderful sounds with so rudimentary a bow: it was made of a small branch to which horsehairs had been crudely attached. I was amazed at his dexterity. I went back to the house where we were staying and took one of my three gold-mounted, gold-tipped Sartory bows. Returning to the market, I gave it to the young Gypsy as a present. He was quite taken aback by so unexpected a gift. I still wonder what ever became of that violinist…and also what became of the bow!

Nowadays the Pernambuco wood used traditionally in bow making is sometimes replaced by carbon fiber, and some manufacturers are even opting for artificial hair. The carbon fiber can yield acceptable results. However I remember a concert given by Bronislaw Huberman in Paris many years ago. He had decided to play with synthetic horsehair. The effect was curious, because he continually had to apply rosin to his bow and produced a cloud of white dust each time.

Rosin, to which I have made only passing reference, is part of the violinist's life and daily rituals. Made from pine resin, originally produced at Colophon in Asia Minor, it is indispensable for the

*H*ere is a rudimentary violin, astonishing in its simplicity, moving in its primitive rusticity. It is a kind of small *sarangi*, which this Nepalese poet and musician probably made with his own hands, using whatever materials and tools he had available. We are far from the sophisticated material and fabrication of our Western violins. Here there is no place for the precious woods of Pernambuco, the horsehairs selected one by one, the secret varnish recipes of the Cremona violin makers. This is a world where there are no teachers and where each player learns by imitating the best players around. Theory gives way to organic learning. This fundamentally popular art is characterized by the immmediacy of an innate and natural way of playing and the pleasure of inventing music and playing for people —spontaneity in its pure state.

rubbing function of horsehair: the rosin gives the hair the stickiness it needs to grab the strings of the violin. If the hairs of a bow are rubbed with soap, no sound would be produced at all. The sound is produced by the frictional effect of these thousands of little roughnesses tugging at the string and letting it go again. Obviously, all this is invisible to the naked eye, but this combined action of string and rosin acts like thousands of little fingers executing a kind of continuous *pizzicato* on the string. This is what generates the string's continuous vibration. It is from this microscopic mechanism that the voice of the violin is born.

*E*mptiness could almost be a synonym for listening: when we want to hear something better, when we want to capture the tiniest sounds of our environment, our immediate impulse is to hold our breath—as if the fact of not breathing and the sense of internal emptiness it creates makes us more permeable to outside vibrations. So there is such a thing as an inner void. But there is also an external void, made up of silence and the transparency of air, far removed from the din of cities, which permits vibration to develop in space; everything can be touched by the sound waves. Our ears, our entire bodies, and all things both animate and inanimate quiver in their contact with this extraordinary vibrating dilation of the air.

FROM EMPTINESS TO VIBRATION

*J*ust as music is generated by resounding against something, sound is set in motion by emptiness, by a hollow. A hollow is a bounded space containing air. The resonating capacity of a hollow depends on its material, its shape, its size and thus can vary from the mouth to various other resounding cavities in our head and thorax from which the sound is amplified and projected on a body of air. Emptiness is thus a pre-requisite to communication. The quality of the material, of a violin or even of a dried pumpkin, is what allows the object to give a recognizable sound, different from any other in its uniqueness. The bounded space should never be touched and certainly never filled. Any impediment to its free vibration destroys the quality or suffocates it completely. We all know how to stop vibration, by touching the vibrating object; thus there is an element of the immaterial, the free and the responsive in this bounded hollow. It already has a character because it gives out a recogniz-able sound, but beyond that it is waiting to re-sound, to respond, to answer back. The same principle holds for the performer or singer who is also an instrument. There can be no rigidity in singing, nor in the playing of its nearest relation, the stringed instrument. Is this not a profound lesson? For we now know that we can only guide and mold the sound, and that the *anima*, the resonating hollow, must be allowed to resonate freely. Thus guidance for melody, freedom for resonance.

Bounded space fulfils two purposes: the ampli-fication of sound and the generation of thought. I somehow cannot conceive of thought being generated

Yin and yang express the duality and complementarity that are to be found in all things: light and shade, male and female, spiritual and material, positive and negative. We are all familiar with the standard representation of yin and yang, which shows a circle divided by a curving line into two equal parts, one white and the other black. In fact this unity is not static: in a more dynamic and productive representation, the reciprocity of yin and yang is portrayed in the form of a triple scroll, the result of a cyclical unfolding, the perfection of a spiral. Duality becomes trinity in a dialectic portrayed here in the brightest of colors, a continuous changing roll of reds, greens, and blues. It is the presence, the projection, of this third element which reconciles the other two.

in dense matter: the atoms and molecules must know dance and space. Emptiness, or the bounded hollow, is also the theater for the play of forces. Of matter, we know that it is imprisoned light, and of light that it is liberated matter and that there is nothing in nature which is only matter. We live within pace and motion best expressed by the concepts of yin and yang, the inhalation and exhalation, the attraction and repulsion, the play of forces without which there can be no expression or creative activity. The ancient philosopher Lao-Tzu insists that it is the space between the spokes of the wheel, the space within a room which allows us to recognize the character and purpose of the wheel or the room. While space is a container for everything that lives and pulsates, it is also a creative agent which needs its own area of activity.

In chapter 11 of the *Tao Tê Ching* ("Teaching of Tao"), Lao-Tzu expresses the essential role of emptiness in a clear and striking fashion:

> Thirty rays converge on the hub,
> but it is the emptiness at the midpoint
> which makes the wheel move.

> One fashions clay to make vases,
> but it is on the internal emptiness
> that their usage depends.

> A house is pierced by doors and windows.
> Once again it is the emptiness
> which permits habitation.

> Being gives possibilities,
> it is by nonbeing that one uses them.

*I*n order to compensate for their lack of space—to forget that they live on an island with a land horizon endlessly limited by mountains, where the land ends abruptly at the sea's edge—the Japanese have become masters in the art of creating illusions of infinity. From the minuscule they create the immense, and with fullness they convey a feeling of emptiness. Here, in a world saturated with mineral and vegetal elements, and with only a small amount of sky, a Zen monk with his walking staff conveys to us the profound serenity inspired by his meditation. The emptiness with which he fills himself gives this painting a center of gravity that attracts and soothes.
A silk painting by Manotobu. *Zen Monk in a Landscape Near a Waterfall*. Tokyo, National Museum.

The Zen garden is the highest expression of the Japanese art of space and illusion. The arrangement of stones and pebbles, representing the element of eternity, and the trace of the rake on the gravel, which gives the illusion that no foot has ever trodden here, combine to create a sense of the infinity of time and space awaiting the new and creative now—the disturbance of a footprint as a skier on fresh snow. This garden at the Daisen-in temple in Kyoto offers itself to the imagination of the monk as he sits in meditation. His meditation is enhanced by the secret joy, familiar to explorers and early morning skiers, of discovering a space that is virgin, unique, and protected.

Thus it is through emptiness, or the readiness to receive (in ordinary language curiosity and learning) that each object or being achieves fullness. Fullness is not meant as a static condition but rather as an endless process of sensing, absorbing, listening, or learning.

It is interesting that in both China and Japan there is little clutter and a maximum of economy in their styles of painting. Traditional Japanese rooms too are largely denuded of furniture which would only take up space. The silk sleeping clothes are rolled up and put away every morning. There are no seats, only low tables, as the Japanese live on the *tatami*, (tightly woven, sweet smelling straw) on the floor. There may be only one object to decorate the room, and if the family acquire more, they simply replace one with another, so that full attention can be given to the one object. We in the West seem obsessed with the idea of filling every emptiness we can capture. Emptiness of space is crowded with possessions of every kind. There is very little sense of space in the average European or American house, however, modern architecture is beginning to recognize the exhilarating use of space and light. We strive to find empty moments which we fill instantly with sound and noise, rather than allowing thought, poetry and music to be conjured by the tranquillity of emptiness. Piped electronic music surrounds us, trying to make us better customers and certainly less reflective, more malleable beings, leaving no silence to protect our uniqueness.

We depend totally on the spaces in our lungs, hearts, arteries, and brains for air. However the habits of living in the first world—the over-consumption of

*L*ake Tahoe in California—my first "experience of emptiness." In a boat, at the onset of dusk, I experienced that moment of total suspension during which nature no longer dares move, as if holding its slightest breath. Between the buzzing of the day's activities and the obscure descent into night there are moments of mystery during which dogs and wolves become one in the silence of the fading light. Silence is the founding element of all thought: it links us to the universal, to the infinite, and to the vital center of our being.

refined foods in particular—lead to a physical and spiritual clogging of our bodies. Those who cannot go beyond the immediate satisfactions of taste, who continue to munch and chew their way through the day, just as those who are saturated with extraneous noise, can never know the quiet emptiness which brings us close to the universal and the infinite.

I once found myself in the midst of a quiet emptiness. As a boy of eight or nine, with a wonderful man Sydney Ehrman, I took a rowboat at dusk on to the open space of Lake Tahoe in California, at an altitude of some 6,000 feet. There was a total stillness which imposed itself on nature, man and animal, even trees, and there was not a whiff of wind. It created a mood which prompted me to say that the very first thought must have happened at the moment the French refer to as "entre chien et loup," between the predators of day and night—that moment of suspense when the day departs and darkness takes over. These are the moments of stillness, quiet, space, void which generate thought and communication.

FILLING THE EMPTINESS

*T*he word "emptiness" is initially misleading: what we perceive as empty is actually air, filled with imperceptible vibrations and energies. Even in a vacuum, movement can occur: for example, the linear motor is a magnetic drive within a vacuum which simply moves the train from one magnet to another, operating at the highest speeds. Thus vacuums, voids, bounded hollows, can form the very fabric, the very design and structure of life.

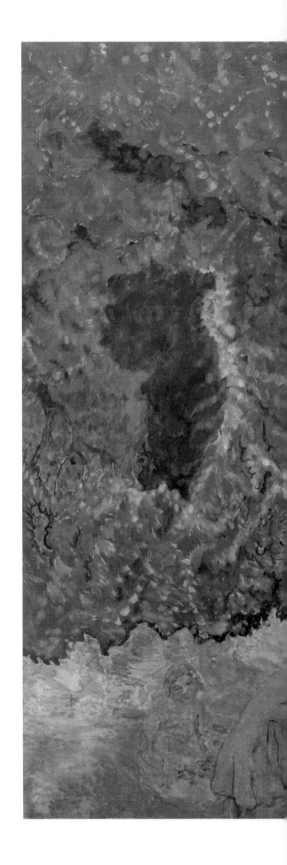

*T*he siesta is that small moment
of emptiness during which
we withdraw from the day
in order to relax and recharge
our energies. In this picture,
the intense heat renders
the shade of the trees irresistible.
Pierre Bonnard (1867–1947),
Summer of 1917.
Saint-Paul-de-Vence,
Fondation A. Maeght.

Nevertheless, the human being always seems eager to escape the void. People feel compelled to speak, and they will say almost anything, however silly, to break the silence. The small pauses in conversation, inactivity during a day's work, or the silence of a deserted house are tiny manifestations of the infinite which we too often find disturbing and try to avoid, it would seem, at all costs.

Our reactions to and behavior within the world of sound and silence is the work of Murray Schafer, a Canadian composer, who is also a wonderful, inspiring teacher. He has invented the new science he calls "soundscape," a term which defines the study of the aural environment in which we find ourselves,

Bicycles in the streets of Shanghai. A sign of urban density and human busyness, yet they present an orderly and rather well-behaved spectacle: there is nobody trying to overtake the person in front. Equanimity and calm are the order of the day. The riot of color created by the plastic raincoats contrasts with the calm, orderly progress of the cyclists. The music of their bicycle bells is a lot less aggressive than the roaring engines and tooting horns of cars in the West.

whether urban, rural, or even of the various times and places stretching back over hundreds of years. Normally we are not aware of the noises which reach us in urban surroundings; they have no "signal value" according to Schafer, whether they consist of general traffic noise, the sound of drilling, or machinery in a factory. As he explained to me, the Native American, walking across his lands, would find significance, or "signal value," in every sound that reached his ears. The vibrations of nature provided information about the humidity, the strength and direction of the wind, the presence of animals, or a thousand other occurrences. This induces a state of constant listening. Today our conversation encourages the deadening of our aural perception and leads to a constant desire to escape this meaningless noise.

This illustrates the importance of valuing the particular over the many, quality over quantity, space over density, peace of mind over mad anxiety. It is a neglect of these values which no doubt contributes to violence, thoughtlessness and aggression. It seems absurd to suggest that a music student needs a sound-proofed room in which to practice when we could so easily transform our environment so that we can once again hear the natural sounds beyond our windows. I always feel that music belongs in natural space and when I played in an enormous hall on the island of Hawaii during World War II it was a delight to watch the birds flying in and out, perching on the rafters. This may not suit every kind of musical taste but it is preferable to the totally isolated rehearsal cells in our modern purpose-built conservatories.

*A*gainst this contemporary cacophony it was an enlightening experience to find myself with my wife Diana in India for the first time in 1951, immersed in a civilization which has retained close links with its historical origins. Indian music and their arts are still regarded as religious offerings, and when we visited in the 1950s the performers were only just beginning to come to terms with the fixed time slots demanded by the broadcasting studios. Indian music deals with the infinite, knowing neither beginning nor end. It emerges imperceptibly from the tuning of the instrument which lays the ground for the particular *raga* or scale to be used. It is part and parcel of a given time of day, mood, or event, whether harvest, wedding, death,

The window is an opening on the world, giving access from the internal to the external. Thanks to windows, we do not need to shut ourselves in if we want to think, dream, or meditate: all we have to do is look at what is happening outside. Within the frame of the window, life's great spectacle is played out. In many modern buildings in our large cities, however, people are obliged to work in windowless rooms, with no visual contact with the external world. What a relief it must be to be able to sit on the ledge of an open window, poised between one's own world and the world outside—the closed and the open, the private and the public. It is sad that in our urban environment we often work emprisoned in soundproofing and air conditioning. Otto Franz Scholderer (1834–1902), *Violinist at the Window*, 1861. Frankfurt, Städelsches Kunstinstitut.

victory or defeat. Indian music belongs to the people who have always played on instruments, which in the early days were simplified forms of the wondrously fashioned instruments of the classical tradition. Folk music is improvised and not read—there is thus always an element of creating, of responding to the needs of the moment and of the player. In the great players this produces an intellectual command and an emotional abandon which is beyond belief. It is as if an intense spiritual upheaval joined forces with the infinite calculating capacity of a computer to express a deep emotion which is universal and true.

In Indian music the choice of *talas* or rhythmic patterns is as varied as the choice of melodic variations. This music is all-inclusive and demands a high level of concentration from the listener. The training of the Indian musician is most exacting: it must begin at a very early age and encompasses the learning of numerous scales each with its own laws, the particular kind of *appoggiatura*, or grace notes required, and a particular number of *talas*, the rhythmic seed. On top of this knowledge the musicians evolve through improvization. They understand better than anyone that liberty can only be achieved after a great many disciplines have been imposed. Liberty means the freedom to achieve results which are inspiring and compatible with the living requirements of the people they belong to. In opening on to another culture, we find one of the routes that will enable us to reconnect with the experience of void and plenitude. Against the pressures of a world that seeks to lock us into monocultures, into a one-dimensional and one-way life, the act of understanding and opening ourselves to other arts of living is like having an inexhaustible oxygen supply, as well as a way of escaping the madness and barbarism that lie in wait for us otherwise.

*I*n Indian music, the function of the *tambura* (nearly always played by a woman) is to support the singers or other instrumentalists with the absolute intervallic measure of a perfect fifth. This basic, automatic, and organic calculation based on the minimum friction between two notes, is made by our ears, which have the ability to distinguish the size of an interval in the same way that our two eyes use triangulation to evaluate the distance which separates us from an object.

EMPTINESS AND THE VIOLIN

*T*he violin has no mechanical content, it waits, empty. But it is also strung and thus not altogether passive; it waits to amplify whatever will fall into its aura.

Because it has no mechanism the violin is highly adjustable by the player, and the player generally follows his or her own instinct to tune the instrument to perfect fifths. Each of the four strings has a character akin to the different registers of the human voice. The perfection of the fifth, exactly three times the speed of the basic note, gives a richness and stability to the intervals of our harmonic music. Those people who feel inimical to the piano naturally miss that perfect fifth, as it would be impossible to apply natural perfect pitch to the piano's tempered scale.

Since for the violinist, the ear is the only guide— as it is for singers—the empty space of the ear and the empty space of the violin combine and meet in an

intangible dialogue, an intimate conversation as swift and imperceptible as the movement of light.

The violin is an instrument that can be played by the blind, as can the human voice, whilst the keyboard only to a limited extent, and best by those fabulous improvising jazz pianists. In playing the violin, vibrations are transmitted through the collarbone and fingers of the right hand which holds the bow. The whole idea is to hold the violin lightly enough not to impede the vibrations even of the bow-stick. The ear is thus the very center of control and all we have said about the importance of listening applies to the violinist to the maximum extent. Very often, just as we are inured to our own mistakes and do not notice them, violinists may not hear themselves playing out of tune until it is pointed out. This is not because of a failure of hearing, but the result of a bias, or of an effort which imposes physical requirements which the violinist cannot meet—perhaps a shrinking of the muscles out of fear or tension which results in playing at a higher pitch than if one were relaxed. A recording is sufficient to reveal this, but it is surprising how tenacious certain violinists' prejudices can be. In the face of conclusive evidence some are still unwilling to accept that some-

A visit to a violin maker's
workshop is always a moving
experience since one can
follow and understand
the different stages
in a violin's gestation.
On the far left we see
an almost completed sound
board. Next to it, a neck
on which the peg box
and scroll have already
been mounted; in the foreground
is a "form" or "mold."

thing is wrong with them. Of course those few will never become great violinists and it is probably useless to try to rid them of this prejudice.

Even before the violin is picked up and held against the musician's body, someone else has already listened to the instrument's empty space to gauge its potential fullness of sound. The violin maker is perhaps one of the supreme magicians of the void, shaping the enclosed space of the violin so that it is filled with the finest sounds of honey and gold that the human ear can ever imagine. It is the violin maker who

*E*ach element of the violin informs the violin maker of its own voice. In combining these various resonances, the violin maker seeks to assemble an instrument whose parts will vibrate in harmony. The French word for a violin maker—*luthier*—originally meant a "maker of lutes," because he once made a whole range of stringed instruments, both plucked as the lute, and bowed as the violin. Over the centuries, the French and the Italians have kept this name, whereas the English use "violin maker," as do the Germans (*Geigenbauer*). There is no doubt that the violin is a melodic instrument, the bow lending it uninterrupted breath. The plucked instruments like the guitar are usually accompaniments to the voice. For the exceptional player, the guitar is also a solo instrument which combines melody with a rhythmic and harmonic accompaniment.

determines the instrument's dimensions, proportions, and curves; makes the varnish to dress the wood; and selects that wood, sometimes even while it is still on the tree—Guarneri tells how the great Stradivari once confided to him that he used to hear "great red fir trees making the air vibrate like a tuning fork." Thus the sound that comes quivering from the strings of a violin is created by the conjoined and complicitous actions of many ears. It is born of a succession of voids, a communication of spaces and sensibilities open to the music that animates it.

*J*ust as Indian music is geared to the perfect fifth and therefore must forego harmony quite deliberately, we in the West have succumbed to the lures of harmony, and we have accepted the fact that no modulation can be possible between dissonant keys unless a formula for compatibility is found. Indian music progresses in perfect fifths, but here twelve successive-fifths do not return exactly to the point of origin. The Pythagorean comma—discovered at about the same time by Pythagoras and ancient Chinese civilization—defines the difference between the note of origin and the note on which we end the cycle of twelve perfect fifths, a cycle which in Indian music proceeds as an infinite spiral, rather than a series of circles. This is a curious phenomenon by which twelve times three times the speed of a given note results in a note which when divided by the square root of twelve yields a note slightly higher than the original one. Thus twelve times three times the original note produces a note which when divided by twelve is not identical with the note of departure. We can adjust this difference by dividing it by twelve, distributing each Pythagorean

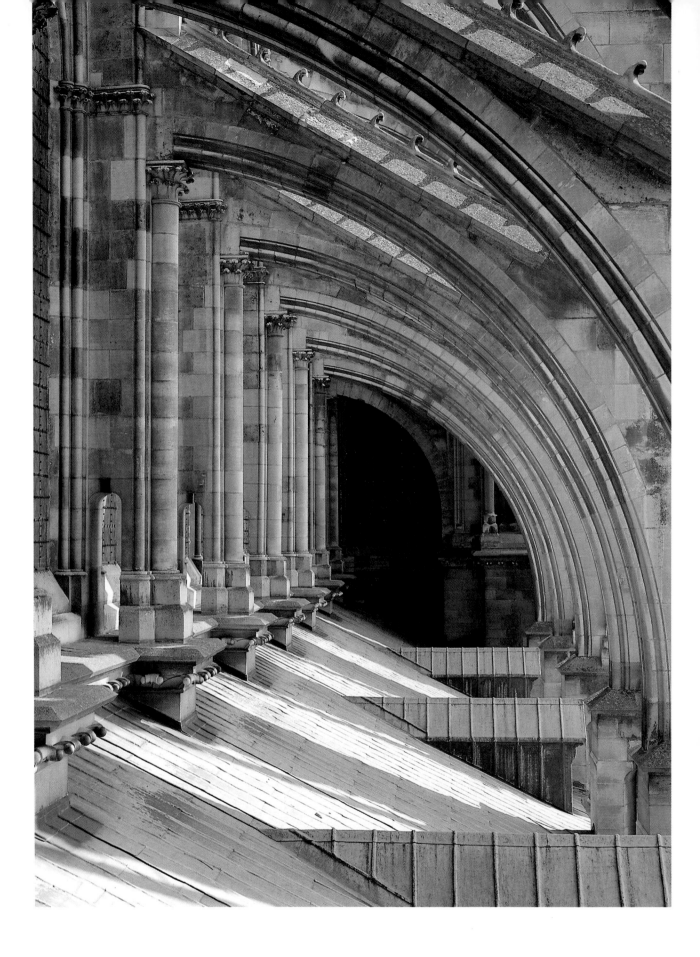

*T*all, narrow buildings, Gothic cathedrals were created in an attempt to reach closer to God through height, yet they also fulfilled the impulse to create bigger and bigger resonating spaces in which the human voice and the voice of the organ could rise to the heavens. The arch represents the triumph of form over empty space, and the invention of the flying buttress enabled medieval architects to realize this grandiose ambition. Without flying buttresses there could be no soaring naves, and without such naves, worshippers could not conceive of the great infinity that both separated them from and united them with their God. Then there is the rainbow, which in all civilizations symbolizes the bridge between earth and the sky, the Hebrew Ark of the Covenant, Noah's ark, Cupid's bow and its arrow of love, the musical bow, the violin bow. In all its forms, whether real or symbolic, the arc or bow represents in some way the ultimate conquest of the void. Reims, seen from the buttresses of the nave of Notre-Dame, south side.

comma divided by twelve and subtracting this one-twelfth from each perfect fifth. As soon as we employ a third note (harmony) our ear can be deceived into accepting a tempered fifth which imposes an out-of-tune interval on our ears. In this way we can indeed modulate between the most distant keys and the basic one of the work. Only rarely are we made aware of how "out of tune" our Western music is, and this affects our thinking and peace of mind. But as soon as a voice, a stringed instrument, or a wind instrument play alone, the musician automatically plays the true fifth. Only the keyboard remains obdurate. Perhaps the new electronic keyboards will overcome this handicap and give us true fifths wherever possible.

There is a remarkable French tuner, Serge Cordier, who has studied the tuning of keyboards and its history over hundreds of years, and has published several books on the subject. Whenever I can, particularly when I am in Montpellier where Cordier lives and works at the university, I ask him to tune the piano I use. He has perfected a way of making the octave rather than the fifth bear the brunt of the tempering, the octave being a much stronger interval than the fifth, which is thus left less distorted by this process. It is a wonderful form of tuning which I highly recommend.

In playing the violin the sound is determined first by the ear, whereas in the piano the pianist's skill in listening for the pitch is very rudimentary, as he must become inured to the discrepancy. Our harmony is in a way the occupation of the space between the notes which would otherwise be left empty. Eventually Western harmony became so dense that the dodeca-phonists felt it their duty to establish order: this involved a kind of "police" order, in which one is not allowed to use the same note twice in a twelve-tone row! Once a line of twelve tones is adopted they are equal and must stay in the same order. Unsurprisingly this comes from an age that wanted to impose by legislation. It has produced masterpieces—the human mind often works best under restraints—but sometimes chaos ensues, as intervals are by nature unequal.

Dissonance used to be expressed as *appoggiatura*, a note so close to the stronger that it cannot escape its resolution, its absolution as it were, but distant enough to be recognized as a melodic interval. The tempered scale introduces a built-in dissonance, as the fifths are not true. This reached its culmination in certain densities which were neither harmonious nor disharmonious, or rather they were disharmonious in the sense that harmony was applied with a thick brush. This led to a form of music where dissonances remain suspended without resolution: we have become used to it and it even has a certain charm.

The emotions aroused by music depend on dissonance in the terms defined and practiced in the Middle Ages, and long, long before. The medieval notion of perpetual resolution is still a source of emotional reaction which is not generated by the major chord. The major implies security, compatibility, optimism and contentment. The reason why a minor chord evokes sadness is that the minor third is in direct dissonance with an implied major third, the third overtone of the tonic, and therefore in competition with it. If in C major the E is not played and E flat is inserted we have harmony. But E flat is in dissonance with the implied overtone which is E, the third overtone of C, two octaves higher, and this carries its own series of dissonant overtones in relationship to C major. To

*A*s intermediary beings between God and the world, angels are, in their own way, a bridge between humanity and heaven. Their message is often addressed in musical form, and there are many instances of vaults and portals of churches (at Santiago de Compostella, for instance) featuring musician angels. The angels in this painting, rather than play on brass instruments that thunder out the news of divine intervention, are represented as a charming, dreamy-faced quintet. A small organ in the center and a *rebec* to the left accompany other angels, who are probably singing. The *rebec* is a distant cousin of the violin, even though it resembles a lute. It probably derives from the Arab *rebab*, and the delicate ornamentation of its sound hole certainly suggests Eastern origins.
Stefano da Verona
(c. 1374–after 1438),
Musician Angels.
Venice, Museo Correr.

maintain a sad emotion the dissonance is prolonged before resolution, very like the inescapable desire to torment a sore tooth with the tongue!

Because the fifth was generally played in its purity and perfection until the advent of the tempered scale, even the organ and keyboard instruments were tuned to perfect fifths, so they could only play the key in which they were tuned, and one or two either side (if tuned in C major then G major or F major). But even then the notes of a fifth above or a fifth below would not be in tune. The violin could flexibly adjust as do all Indian stringed instruments by tuning to a given key. The Italians call this *scordatura*, whereby certain strings are tuned to a different note to play a particular composition. For example in Mozart's beautiful E flat major *Symphony Concertante for Violin and Viola*, the viola is tuned half a note higher so that the top string is B flat instead of A, the D becomes E flat, etc. The viola sounds so much better in this *scordatura* and the piece is certainly much easier to play in that key than when tuned ordinarily. Unfortunately most viola players prefer not to "untune" their instrument but to play it in its original tuning, which not only makes the piece harder to play but also diminishes the sonority of the viola.

For these reasons, the violinist should be allowed to express a degree of intuition regarding pitch, color, and texture, and should be aware of the tensions between notes. This is quite a different set of talents, more akin to the playing of wind instruments, than to the piano. The violinist seems to live and move in the empty spaces between notes and transforms and fashions them in accordance with his own and the listeners' sensibilities. An artisan of emptiness, the violinist seems to work as much with form as with content.

*H*ere we have a rather different music. Instead of the celestial harmonies of the spheres, there is the dissonant music of death. With one foot resting on an hourglass—symbolic of the passing of time—a skeleton invites the rich man to a last and final dance: a *danse macabre*. In this allegory, death is armed not with a scythe but with a violin. So here the music of the violin takes on diabolic associations. One also finds this dimension of evil in certain works of the violin repertoire, as for example Stravinsky's *The Soldier's Tale*, in which a young soldier sells his soul to the devil, as symbolized by the violin.
Franz Francken the Younger (1581–1641),
The Wicked Rich Man.
Private collection.

In an image of studied disorder,
this picture brings together
several families of bowed
instruments. Propped against
stools and cushions,
we see the *viola da gamba*,
a cousin of the violin,
recognizable by its six strings
and C-shaped sound hole.
In front, on the ground,
a rebec rests its neck across
a *pochette*. To the right,
lying across a musical score,
a *lira da braccio*, and then,
scattered about,
wind instruments,
and various exotic birds.
In the background
of this comfortable, wealthy
interior, a quartet gives
a discreet concert.
Jan Bruegel de Velours
(1568–1625), *Allegory of Hearing*
(detail of musical instruments).
Madrid, Museo del Prado.

*T*he work of the violin maker
is built on patience and delicacy
of touch: with this artisan,
the art of equilibrium reaches
the pinnacle of refinement.

THE VIOLIN MAKER

*I*t is no accident that the art of violin making was
born on the plains of the Po River valley. Italy
has always been the country of melody, because
the Italian language carries song within its vowels just
as the sun carries light. Vowels rule supreme: when
one travels in Italy, one hears only the ringing tones
of the resonating "a," "o," and "i" sounds. They are the
vibrations which flow into the chambers of mouth and
face, enabling us to emit sounds and communicate
with others: without vowels there would be no
sound, without sound there would be no speech, and,
a fortiori, no music. It is around the vowel that the vocal
chords vibrate, and it is the vowel that colors and

amplifies the original vibration. Consonants are merely small pebbles tossed into the flowing sound stream of the voice for accent and punctuation.

ITALY: THE BIRTHPLACE OF VIOLIN MAKING

*B*ecause the Italian language is so intrinsically and fundamentally vocal, music and song are as much second nature to Italians as is their taste for drama and the irresistible warmth of their way of being.

Song and drama fused into opera and became the people's most popular spectacle and heritage. Thus the Italians perfected the further miracle of acoustics, the opera house—that elegant, shallow horse-shoe shape which has remained alongside the violin as our models for a resonating chamber.

In more general and subtle ways, Italy has, since the Renaissance, been the center of Europe's cultural life: from architecture and music to painting and sculpture, it was here that the hearts of all the Muses beat. A trip to Italy was seen as a necessary part of any artist's development. The existence of publishing houses made possible the printing and distribution of music, and the support of wealthy patrons—such as the princely houses of the Medici and the church—assured Italy a place at the heart of Europe's artistic, dramatic, and musical life. As for opera, it was so hugely successful that in the course of just a few years in the seventeenth century several hundred theaters were built for opera in Venice alone. What city today could boast such a count? Even if one took cinemas into account, where would one find such a wealth of culture?

As a result of this enthusiastic abundance, Italian creative artists became known for their talent and skill, and for centuries they were invited to courts all across Europe: in the sixteenth century, Francis I had brought Italian architects to build his castles on the banks of the Loire; he was also the patron of Leonardo da Vinci, one of humanity's towering men—artist, poet, philosopher, and prolific inventor of many things from submarines to flying machines. Later, in the eighteenth century, it was largely Italians who raised glorious St Petersburg, the city of Peter the Great, on once uninhabitable marshlands.

*O*pera first emerged in Italy in the early seventeenth century. The sumptuous decor and spectacular machinery seen here speak of the princely origins of this art of the voice. Italian-style opera houses, with their horseshoe-shaped ground plan, have always provided ideal acoustics: no dryness, no excessive reverberation, but a perfect balance between instruments and voices. This is owing to a vertical pipe-shaped space with little horizontal depth, which traps the sound as it rises from the stage. The enemy of acoustics is the horizontal cinema hall which traps a shaft of light but kills sound. Giovanni Paolo Pannini (c. 1691–1765), *A Celebration Given by Cardinal de la Rochefoucauld at the Argentina Theater in Rome, 15 July 1747, on the Occasion of the Marriage of the Dauphin Louis and Marie-Josèphe of Saxony.* Paris, Musée du Louvre.

*I*n former times, a musician's
patrons were kings, princes,
dukes, and ecclesiastical
dignitaries; then came the private
men of wealth. Bach, Haydn,
Mozart, and Beethoven composed
for religious ceremonies,
entertainments, and celebrations
of major events in the lives
of leading public figures.
Nowadays the patrons
who define the tastes and culture
of our age are usually often
the faceless representatives
of more institutional sources
of funding such as banking
and industry.
Antonio Domenico Gabbiani
(1652–1726),
*Prince Ferdinand de' Medici
with the Musicians
of His Entourage.*
Florence, Palazzo Pitti.

In the musical domain, Italian violinists and singers dominated the cultural life of Europe: the violinist Nardini, for example, emigrated to the court at Stuttgart. Jommelli, and later Salieri, went to Vienna; Lully to Versailles; Locatelli to Amsterdam. That all these musicians traveled to foreign lands bears witness to the incredible wealth of the crucible that was Italy. Culturally, Europe was both varied and integrated: Bach, for instance, knew the works of Corelli and Vivaldi and transcribed many of their works.

This rich peninsula of Italy bounded by sea and mountains, with the untamed Apennine range as its backbone, was ideally suited for the pursuit of beauty

*I*n this painting, *the viola da gamba* is also a still life: the dead game are silent as a result of the hunter's bullet, while the wooden instrument awaits the touch of the expert hand which, as if by magic, will bring it to life. As its name suggests, the *viola da gamba* is held between the legs, unlike the cello, which rests on a spike. Its repertoire reached a high degree of refinement, particularly in seventeenth-century England and in France with Monsieur de Sainte-Colombe and his pupil Marin Marais. Then it was eclipsed by the cello and other instruments of the violin family. François Desportes (1661–1743), *Still life: Game, Fruit and Viola da gamba.* Gien, Château, Musée International de la Chasse.

*L*eft: Juan Oliver (b. 1330), a fresco from Pamplona Cathedral, detail of a female musician. Pamplona, Museo de Navarra.

in all its forms; and, very particularly in this case, for the development of the violin which finally captured the human voice itself. There were other bowed instruments in the world, for example, the rebec, the offspring of the Arabic rebab brought to Europe by the Saracens in the eighth century, which had three strings and a rounded back. There was also the medieval viol, with its six strings and its C-shaped sound holes, an instrument still with us in the form of one of its cousins, the *viola da gamba*.

Sixteenth-century Italy also had an instrument which in a curious sense was a precursor of our violin: the *lira da braccio*. Unlike the *viola da gamba* (literally, the "leg" viola), which was held between the knees, the *lira da braccio* was supported by the arm (*braccio*). The *lira da braccio* or *viola da braccio*, like the violin, had four strings that were tuned in fifths. It was waisted at the midpoint, and, like the violin, had two symmetrical f-shaped sound holes; it differed from the violin in that all its edges and indentations were rounded. This

*H*ere, in an atmosphere
of joyous festivity, we have
the earliest family of violins.
In the center we recognize
the cello. Above it, to the left,
a shy violin, showing only its back.
To the right, more assertively,
a viola. We are still some way
from the Cremonese masters
of the sixteenth
and seventeenth centuries,
and the music these angels
have chosen for their celestial
concert would probably
sound strange to us.
Gaudenzio Ferrari (c. 1475–1546),
Musician Angels
(detail of a fresco).
Saronno, Sanctuario.

entire family of related instruments in all sizes covered the full range of pitch, from high notes to low. At Saronno, in the fresco decorating the cupola of the sanctuary of Santa Maria delle Grazie, one can see this wonderful family represented for the first time, in a celestial concert given by a group of angels. The smallest of these instruments, the *violino piccolo*, also known as the *violino alla francese*, was closest to the evolved violin of the seventeenth century. Maggini Gaspar da Salo and finally the Amati family had yet to produce

their masterpieces before Antonio Stradivari, a disciple of Amati, appeared.

*F*rom the world trading port of Genoa to Venice in that glorious and fertile region at the foot of the Alps, well watered and boasting some of our world's most cultivated and beautiful cities, amid wonderful churches, houses and superb food, violin making flourished, in particular in Cremona, which until then had been best known for its thirteenth-

*T*he trees used for violin making. These young, slender firs, their trunks still slightly frail, will have to wait many years before the violin maker allows them to sing. A fir tree, a pine, or a spruce has to be about two hundred years old before it has a sufficiently large diameter to be used in violin making. It is also only then that it achieves the ideal distance between its growth rings.

These firs are in the Jura mountains, which yield the best woods for producing a fine timbre in an instrument. Once cut and sawed, the pieces have to be left for a few quiet years of drying out (some violin makers say five years, others fifty or more) before they can be worked. Today this process is often by-passed through artificial drying, a most unfortunate lapse.

century bell tower (the highest in Italy). It was here that Andrea Amati was born, and here that, around 1550, he created the modern violin. Following him, his sons Antonio and Girolamo, and particularly his grandson Niccolo Amati, went on to perfect the instrument which would be coveted by both the musicians and the aristocracy of Europe.

Cremona must have been particularly well situated: it had woods of fir spruces, a good climate and the gifted craftsmen required to fashion a violin. The craft of violin making thus begins in the forest. The violin maker comes here to choose the trees from which his violins will be crafted, reserving the timber he will be using, twenty years later, to make his instruments. They say that in those days violin makers identified the trees that would be capable of singing by hitting them with a mallet and listening to the vibration carried within each tree.

Spruce, pine, fir, and maple may be used for the backplate, ribs, neck, and bridge, while ebony, a particularly hard wood from Africa is used for the fingerboard and pegs. The ingredients of those frequently secret formulas used in the magnificent varnishes were often imported from the Orient with which the region was in direct trading relations.

The climate was ideal for seasoning woods and drying the varnished instruments. Houses here often had a high terrace, covered and airy—known as the *aerium*. There the violins were put out to dry as the successive layers of different varnishes were applied, sometimes up to thirty. This is an excellent example of the slow and meticulous metamorphosis that transforms the chrysalis of this resonating wooden box into a wonderful musical butterfly, a process that also highlights the importance of the quality of the climate, of the air temperature and humidity.

An infinite combination of barely definable factors is involved in violin making, and even today we can hardly match the superb achievements of those great masters whose names have become synonymous with excellence.

*T*he varnishes used by the master violin makers of the past still remain a mystery: nobody has ever been able to reproduce their depth of color and transparency—rather like the stained glass in church windows, whose secrets have also been lost. However, we do have today highly sophisticated techniques. Varnishing is not some banal chemical process; it is a scientific operation in which the choice of ingredients and their mixing, cooking, and drying are all equally crucial, and it requires one to be something of a wizard. Violin making school, varnishing room. Cremona, Palazzo Raimondi.

loa Sadl inv et fingit   GENES IIII

THE GREAT VIOLIN MAKERS

It was within this exceptional environment that the
art of violin making grew and flourished. Within
a short time, Cremona, followed by the neighboring
town of Brescia, was producing violins for orchestras
all over Italy. Niccolo Amati trained eminent pupils:
Ruggieri, Andrea Guarneri, the great-uncle of the
famous Guarneri del Gesù, and, of course, Antonio
Stradivari. These violin makers signed their violins
inside the instrument, on a label visible through
the left f-hole and stuck to the backplate, giving
their name, the year and place of manufacture in Latin
form. So Stradivari became Stradivarius and Guarneri
became Guarnerius.

The label inside my "Prince Khevenhüller" for
example bears Stradivari's inscription in Latin "made
in my ninetieth year," a fact of which he must have
been very proud.

Giuseppe Antonio Guarneri (1698–1744) occu-
pies a rather special position among the great names
of violin making. He was the most distinguished of a

*C*hapter 4

of the Book of Genesis,

which describes Cain's murder

of Abel, says that Jubal,

one of Cain's descendants,

was the inventor of music.

The engraver here has chosen

to illustrate this brief reference

by representing Jubal

as the ancestor of violin makers.

In his workshop are stacked

all kinds of instruments,

and each craftsman

is fully absorbed in his task,

while groups of nymphs

and cupids dance to the sound

of violin, flute, and bagpipes.

Maarten de Vos (1532–1603),

illustration of Genesis, chapter 4.

Paris, Bibliothèque Nationale

de France.

famous family of violin makers. The quality of his work was inspired and often impetuous, each piece was the fruit of a specific inspiration. Guarneri periodically modified his models, so that each of his violins was and still is an original creation, an instrument that speaks another language from that of its brothers. Indeed, one can hardly identify particular periods of his work, as each violin is a masterpiece in itself and does not conform to its predecessor. Looking at his sketches, one can sometimes sense the man's impatience. To emphasize the divine inspiration he felt,

Guarneri signed his violins with the initials IHS (*Iesus Hominum Salvator*), or "Joseph Guarnerius del Jesu." He was a genius, more rustic and down-to-earth than the disciplined Stradivari, and formerly not as recognized as Stradivari. Today Guarneri's instruments are even more highly prized than Stradivari's, and there are far fewer. My own Guarnerius del Jesu, the "Lord Wilton" is perhaps the most coveted instrument in the world .

The career of Antonio Stradivari (1644–1737) is exactly the reverse of Guarneri's. He was meticulous,

*S*tradivarius violins are treasures.

If not actually played

they are lovingly sheltered

from public view,

and exhibited from time

to time to give people

an idea of how beautiful

a violin can be.

Here one can admire

the distinguished aristocratic

profiles of three

of the approximately

four hundred extant examples

of the great Cremona violin

maker's art.

New York, The Metropolitan

Museum of Art.

industrious, and extremely demanding, as much with himself as with the materials he used. Throughout his long life, he pursued a quest for the absolute. Stradivari subjected himself to constant self-criticism, and even destroyed a number of violins with which he was not entirely satisfied. He spent several years seeking out the ideal wood for his violins. Then he kept studying the shape and curves that would produce the greatest beauty of sound. Finally, around age fifty, he reached the pinnacle of his art. He had found the perfect balance of materials, curvatures, and varnish. He was to live for another forty-one years, never ceasing to create these wonders of acoustics we still find so moving today.

Although the art of making violins reached its apogee in Italy, it had already developed notably in many countries of Europe, from the eastern Slav countries to Spain and England. But by the seventeenth century, Jacobus Stainer, working in Absam near Innsbruck, was proving a worthy rival to the Lombard masters, whose work he must have known. He was the greatest of the early German violin makers. In the nineteenth century at Mirecourt in France and Mittenwald in Bavaria distinguished schools of violin making were established. Modern contemporary violin making is pursued globally in Europe and America, Japan, China and South America. To meet the demand for cheap instruments for the beginner the Chinese have produced quarter- and half-size violins and bows which come with strings and even an instruction manual! This may seem dreadful but for their purposes they are not bad—they can be played and at least they are in wood and not metal, unlike the first violin I stamped on in anger at the age of three.

These artisans of Cremona and Brescia, some of whom were later to move to Milan (Grancino, for instance) and Venice (Santo Serafin), already enjoyed considerable fame in their own lifetimes. They were often quite rich, and because of their reputations they could command the high prices their instruments deserved.

For a long time violin prices were stable, but today prices are dictated by the accumulated cost of maintenance, insurance, inflation, rarity, fragiliy, and value as an investment. A very great instrument commands extremely high prices today; but like other great works of art, many are bought at auction by people who, while they may genuinely cherish the instrument, are not performers, the latter being frequently unable to afford such instruments.

Fortunately the modern violin maker is producing extremely satisfactory violins in almost every country, violins which are far more affordable and usually more robust than the surviving eighteenth- and nineteenth-century instruments.

I admire some of these contemporary violin makers and do my best to encourage their work in this most exacting and beautiful craft. Among modern violin makers may I cite in particular the French violin maker Étienne Vatelot, the violinist's greatest ally and friend. I would like to encourage this profession, because, like many other crafts, it is being suffocated by our industrial civilization. I also believe that the

We admire the violin, we listen to it, we play it, we touch it. It is beautiful and full of history, dreams, and promises. But only the great violin maker understands the instrument from the inside. Étienne Vatelot is one of these, and he can care for and defend the violin—even against the violinist, if necessary. He concerns himself with the violin's body and soul. He is every violinist's confidant and ally, and I am one of many who owe him a debt of gratitude. From left to right: Alain Meunier, Mstislav Rostropovitch, Étienne Vatelot, Salvatore Accardo, Franco Petracchi, Régis and Bruno Pasquier.

violin maker's craft would bring great satisfaction to many young people who have the gifts of intuition, intelligence, esthetic sensibility, judgment and a keen ear. As a result of the demands of violinists, contemporary violin makers can truly be motivated in their vocation. The same talents are also used to maintain in good repair the violins of the past. Because of their value, we are today treating these violins with much greater respect than some of the "vandal" violin repairers of the nineteenth and early twentieth centuries.

MY VIOLINS

The work of the violin maker is extraordinarily complex and therefore difficult to reproduce. The manufacture of an object with no straight lines and no flat surfaces, the assembly of seventy-odd pieces which must only be glued together, this process in which each action proceeds from an almost mystical inspiration—all this still belongs to the fragile and secret world of artisanry. Not only is the player inspired by the instrument but the instrument responds to the player. That is why each violin has its own character, and leaves its mark on the person playing it, like a close companion. I once had the chance to borrow the Guarnerius belonging to Eugène Ysaÿe which was then in the care of Émile Français. This was in the early 1930s and the instrument seemed to me as if it played itself; it interpreted the work as if it were still in Ysaÿe's hands. Today this instrument belongs to Isaac Stern.

For myself, I acquired my first beautiful Italian violin at the age of eight. It was a seven-eighths Grancino, not a full-size instrument. This was in 1924 when some kind friends of my father paid eight hundred dollars. I have never parted with that instrument.

*T*he violin maker is the father of the violin, the one who begets it and brings it forth into the world. He is also its doctor: he has the ear, eye, and hand that repair, adjust, and sometimes even restore life to a violin. An intimate relationship inevitably develops between the violinist and the violin maker or luthier, because the latter is consulted not only at the moment of acquisition, but right through the life of a violin, and right through the career of the violinist as well. One hopes that the young apprentices in this workshop in Cremona will have the talent and perseverance to become great violin makers, on a par with my dear Étienne Vatelot. A recent exhibition of contemporary violin making in Paris was organized by Vatelot to great success, and he himself is an authority and author on the art of bow making.

The next instrument, my first full-size, was another Grancino, bought in 1927 at Tournier in Paris on the rue de Rome. This was the violin on which I made my début in New York. For my tour of the United States in the autumn of 1928 I was lent a fine Guarnerius by Wurlitzer—the "Bâle," and by Christmas 1928 I had acquired the "Prince Khevenhüller."

The latter, momentous event occurred when I was twelve and my violin playing career was already under way. Henry Goldman, a music-lover known for his generosity, had heard that I was playing on a borrowed violin, and he invited my father and me to his apartment which overlooked Central Park and the Metropolitan Museum. A very gentle, blind man, he would guide his visitors around his glorious collection of paintings and sculptures, pointing out the smallest detail. I vividly recall him sitting in his armchair, talking to my father and me, his hands hovering near a box of chocolates on one side, and over his cigars on the other.

*T*he position of the hand here is perfect—the well-rounded fourth finger, everything is impeccable. However this instrument—was this the Grancino my parents bought in Paris?—was rather large for the little boy that I then was. Yehudi Menuhin in 1927.

His incredible offer took my breath away: Mr. Goldman wanted me to choose any violin I wanted, whatever the price. It was as if a fairy, or rather a genie, had offered to make my dreams come true. My choice fell on a violin that I had seen a year earlier in San Francisco, a Stradivarius made in 1733. As tradition required, it bore the name of a previous owner: "Prince Khevenhüller."

This was in January 1929, at the time of the Wall Street crash, when the contrast of human destinies—those who had everything and those who had lost everything—could not have been more poignant. Mr. Goldman paid sixty thousand dollars for my violin, and thanks to him, I became the owner of an instrument of impressive proportions. Its roundness and breadth were the source of the sound it produced, which was at once tender and sensual. Its varnish was an ecclestiastical red color as of velvet or dark wine, and had a depth that equalled its sound. The dealer, Emil Herrmann, threw in a complementary Tourte bow, which is now worth twice the price of the violin at that time.

Many years later, in 1952, after my first trip to Japan, I was able to afford the "Soil," a Stradivarius dating from 1714. This period of Stradivarius's life is often referred to as his golden age when he made his most famous violins. The "Soil" is without doubt one of the greatest violins of the world, and its range of color, power and brilliance is quite amazing. It maintains an evenness on all strings, without ever losing its quality. The "Soil" has a purity and warmth of tone which combines with its brilliance in remarkable proportions, enabling the instrument to do justice to every emotion imaginable. It is also a glorious instru-

ment to look at. I lived with that instrument for about thirty years and finally parted with it only when I acquired the "Lord Wilton," yielding the "Soil" to a younger colleague who had coveted it for many decades—Itzhak Perlman.

Although I had spent my life thus far with two very great Stradivarii violins I had always wanted to own and play a Guarnerius as well. The second Guarnerius violin which I played for around a year and a half had been lent to me by a German collector in Brunswick. I had simply looked in the William Hill catalogue of supreme Guarneri, and of all the instruments listed there the one I wanted was the "Count d'Egville." I found out to whom it belonged and flew to Brunswick to meet Herr Lutz, who had quite a collection of outstanding instruments. Although Herr Lutz tried very hard to persuade me to take one of the other instruments, I came away with the "d'Egville." This turned out to be one of the happiest partnerships ever: the violin can be heard on the recording and video I made with Ravi Shankar in New York to mark the twenty-fifth anniversary of the United Nations.

As I was in no position to buy the "Count d'Egville" I finally—reluctantly—relinquished the instrument after a concert at the Paris Opera House with Paul Paray conducting, and the instrument went back to its rightful owner. You can imagine my horror twenty years later when I tracked the violin to a physicist in Boston, and instead of seeing my favorite instrument, I encountered a violin covered with a horrible, hard varnish applied by one of those "vandals" I referred to earlier. My heart fell—this violin had lost its quality of sound and its owner did not seem to understand what had happened to it. Fortunately I

*T*he violin is an instrument of great fragility that needs loving care and attention. I am appalled by the negligence of some violinists, who allow sweat and rosin dust to accumulate on their violins. Right from the start of their studies, children should be taught to respect their instruments. The magical and the dreamlike character of music should not let us forget the almost organic bond between the violinist and the violin.

Yehudi Menuhin in 1929.

persuaded him to let Jacques Français, the son of Émil Français and one of the outstanding dealers, give it to his violin repairer, a craftsman of infinite integrity. After nearly two years, with the patience of Job, having removed microscopically all the offending varnish, he restored the voice and the beauty of the "Count d'Egville."

My last public performance was with a Guarnerius, the very "Lord Wilton" that was my crowning acquisition. I played the Bach double concerto with Gidon Kremer at the opening concert of my Festival in Gstaad in 1995.

In 1630, the theoretician
Pierre Trichet noted, in his
*Traité des instruments
de musique*: "Violins are used
principally for dances, balls,
ballets, masquerades, serenades,
aubades, festivities, and all joyous
pastimes, having been adjudged
more appropriate to these kinds
of pastime than any other
instrument." The role
of the violin as an instrument
for popular entertainment
is clear in these two countryside
scenes. Here the violin
is still at one with Mother Nature;
it has not yet completely
flowed into the mold of salon life.
François Louis Joseph Watteau
(1758–1823), *The Fiddler*.
Lille, Musée des Beaux Arts.
Porcelain from Viana do Castelo,
musician plate,
nineteenth century.
Porto, Museu Nacional
de Soares dos Reis.

THE VIOLIN PLAYER

*I*n its origins, the violin was an instrument of
the people: in villages the violinist's job was
to escort the wedding party and get the guests
dancing—whether in Russia, Poland, Romania, Norway, Scotland, the Blue Mountains of Virginia or the
dancing master with his *pochette* violin in the salons
of France and cultivated Europe. Standing there, feet
tapping out the rhythm, the violinists swept the revel-
ers along with their exhilarating tunes and virtuosity.
There is surely no instrument better suited for marking
the rhythm of dance. Moreover, the violin's brilliance
of tone can be heard even when played in the open air
or in taverns.

At end of the seventeenth century the violin entered the serious classical repertoire and composers discovered its riches and potential, with Corelli, Vivaldi, and others composing concerti especially for the violin. This came about as the audience which listened while seated developed from the active, dancing crowd.

Bach's works for the violin illustrate perfectly its origins as a folk instrument, which belongs not only to the voice but also to the dance. Bach's sonatas consist of four movements: an improvised introduction, the fugue, a slower third movement, and a fast last movement. However the partitas are a separate form which consist exclusively of what were by then stylized dances—the gavotte, minuet, courante, saraband and gigue. Only the last partita in E major has a brilliant prelude which ushers in the dances.

A certain mystique has always accompanied a violinist's command of his instrument and the hearts of his audiences. He was often imbued with supernatural powers and his ability to seduce was perhaps envied by lesser mortals. Paganini was the first violinist to develop an international career, and he wisely did nothing to dispel the rumor of his association with the Devil. Tartini's wonderful *Devil's Trill* Sonata was supposedly inspired by a devil's laughter heard in a dream. And even today when people apply the word "genius" to a so-called "child prodigy" (expressions I have always detested) an echo of the idea of gifts from higher powers remains. This can unfortunately become an easy way for parents and society to neglect their obligations to *all* children.

A CHILD OF THE PEOPLE AND OF DANCE

*T*he strolling fiddlers of yesteryear, the wandering musicians, these heralds of a people's musical language, are the ancestors of violinists. I love to see them depicted in Chagall's canvases: there they are, roaming the highways and byways, moving from village to hamlet, creating joy, and at least temporarily overcoming human prejudices against Gypsy and Jew.

It has taken the solo standing violinist a long time to gain social status, emerging from pure "entertainer" into a fully-fledged literate musician who interprets great and brilliant works for large seated audiences. Works had to become longer to accommodate a seated span of time rather than a dance of shorter duration.

*T*his violinist, dressed in red, has all the astute shrewdness of a beggar: his wanderings from village to village have turned him into a connoisseur of human nature. Here he must be a Jew, accompanied by his son, who appeals to the villagers' generosity. The villagers, however, keep their distance, at once seduced by this wandering entertainer and suspicious. This simple, touching scene represents Chagall's childhood memories of the Russian town of his birth, viewed through the prism of an imagination filled with fantasy, lyricism, and humor. Marc Chagall (1887–1985), *The Violinist*, 1912–13. Düsseldorf, Kunstsammlung Nordrhein-Westfalen.

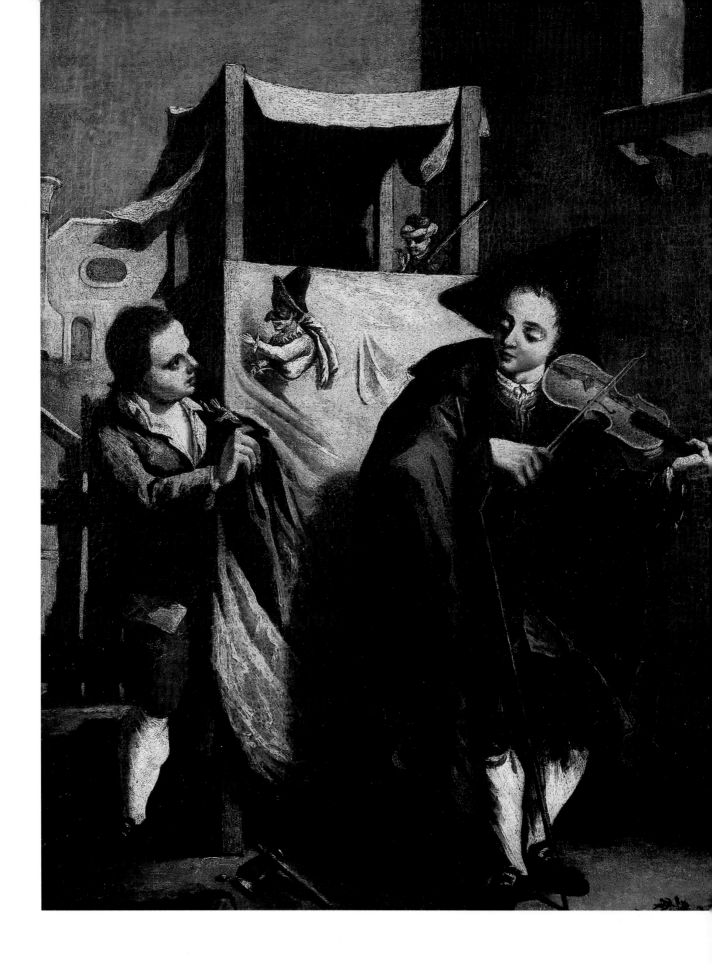

The violinist enjoyed the ambiguous and para-doxical situation of being both a social inferior and gifted with first-class abilities. I suppose standing has always been considered inferior to sitting, and the "seated" instrumentalists (harpsichordists and lute players) enjoyed higher status than the dancing master! Even Mozart had to eat with the servants when playing for the Bishop of Salzburg. The social strata—the castes—had to be severely demarcated to the extent that in England "guests" and musicians belonged to two quite separate categories, and it was only before World War II that this distinction had disappeared.

I am reminded of the story of the great Austrian violinist Fritz Kreisler, who was enjoying tremendous popularity in England. One day he received an invitation from a leading "socialite":

"Mr. Kreisler, may I invite you to dinner at my house tomorrow evening?

"Certainly," he agreed.

"And of course you will be bringing your violin?"

"No," replied Kreisler. "My violin doesn't eat."

*F*ortunately, violinists—and musicians in general—no longer have to endure the state of domesticity which was once their lot. But they should also never forget their roots—the origin of their art in dance, the dance that animated them at harvest time and village weddings, the dance that set their hearts beating to the rhythm of farandoles, gavottes, and jigs. They should continue playing this kind of music on and off stage, from the Scottish fiddler to the interpreters of Bach's solo sonatas and the folk musicians of France and Spain. Thet bring a gaiety and rural simplicity, of which the peasant chorus in Mozart's Don Giovanni (Act I, Scene 7) gives an exquisite image: "Che piacer, che piacer che serà..." ("What pleasures, what pleasures will be"). That chorus was the occasion of an interesting experience at my festival at Gstaad in 1994. I was conducting Mozart's opera in a concert version. The members of the chorus were amateurs, and I asked them to come forward and perform the scene of the marriage of Zerlina and Masetto at the front of the stage, and to allow their bodies to follow the movement of the music. The result was as charming as it was lively, as musical as it was entertaining. For this natural rhythm of the body, which responds to music and dance, creates that suppleness so necessary for the vibration of the sound. Without lightness and flexibility, the notes cannot develop in space and reach

*H*ere we have yet another image of the populist character of the violin as an open-air instrument, played in the country or in the streets and destined for simple folk—Russian peasants in the case of Chagall, or Venetian bystanders, as here. The violin has always been nourished by its folk roots, and this fact should never be forgotten by the violinists of today. Here the violin is associated with a puppet show, punctuating various moments of the action. The position of the violinist's hands is entirely correct, suggesting that the painter himself played the instrument, which would not be surprising, since the violin was very popular in Venice. Domenico Maggiotto (1713–1794), *Puppet Theater in Venice*. Milan, Museo Teatrale alla Scala.

out to the listener. This is a fundamental notion, and I try to convey it to my students: if young violinists were to make the effort to "dance" slightly and unobtrusively while they play, they would more easily free their bodies and overcome their inhibitions. I often meet children who are working hard at their violin playing and who think they are doing the right thing when they hold themselves stiff—and end up being about as expressive as a lamppost.

This is why I would like to introduce the art of dance into my school, not in the refined form of ballroom dancing, but in its more popular aspect, in the shape of Irish, Scottish, Norwegian, and Gypsy dance. The violin should never be allowed to lose contact

*T*his scene, part religious, part profane, is organized around a central character: a woman with lowered gaze, bowing her head slightly, like a Madonna. She has her left hand on her heart, and with her right hand seems to be making a gesture of benediction. Is it directed at the musicians surrounding her, or at the spectator looking at the fresco? Whatever the case, a great peace emanates from this concert scene, which seems dedicated more to meditation than festivity. The violinist stands thoughtfully, watching intently for the lady's reactions. The harp is played by a man, which is fairly unusual. As for the guitarist and the wind player, they listen attentively to each other in order to perfect the harmony that is being woven before our eyes.
Concert Champêtre, fresco decorating a late eighteenth-century chapel. Cuzco, Peru, Museo de Arte Coloniale de Santa Catarina.

with its folk roots. If it denies its past, it becomes dry and lifeless, like an uprooted tree which, if denied its sap, withers and dies.

Interestingly, the folk crucible from which the violin and its music have emerged represents for "civilized" violinists a kind of lost paradise, which they can approach but never completely enter. There is a quality characteristic of violinists of the people—be they Gypsies, Norwegians, or Hungarians—a certain something that simply cannot be imitated, like some jealously guarded secret which only they possess, but which is in fact a distillation of the genetic and the environmental.

During a film directed by Bruno Monsaingeon, I had an interesting encounter with a Hungarian Gypsy violinist. I played first—Sarasate's well-known *Gypsy Airs*—and tried to put myself into it body and soul. Then it was the Gypsy violinist's turn to play the same piece, and we suddenly found ourselves in another world—a world of different colors and different music. The Gypsy added all kinds of wild ornamentation, and, working from Sarasate's original, I realized I could never hope to imitate the genuine article, a whole sound universe, a whole musical landscape with multiple rhythms that surged uncontrollably from the Gypsy's violin. It was as if a whole people—his people—were making their voice and their history heard.

We should respect these cultural riches and traditions handed down from father to son. Our modern civilization has developed such a sense of its own superiority that it tends to disdain anything it considers different. Instead of trying to understand and learn about difference, it attempts to reduce them to our uniformity. It tries to force native peoples—at one time the Native American, today the Indians of Amazonia—to flow into the mold of our "civilization," and to become just like us, murdering them if they resist. These peoples are equal and different and have a great deal to teach us in their turn.

Folk music, and particularly the folk music of Eastern Europe, has always brought a vital, fertile element to Western music. Bela Bartók was one of the most renowned researchers of folk music, able to reach into the Balkan, Turkish, and North African heritage in order to enrich the content of classical music. Zoltán Kodály too drew his music from the singing soul of his country. Beethoven and Mendelssohn succumbed to folk music—in their case Scottish—and were similarly drawn to the one true language which goes beyond the study of music to speak to the heart of emotion.

*I*n the street, even when surrounded by the noise and movement of the crowd, this musician is sheltered and protected by the shell that the song of his violin creates around him. He lives in this inner world, with his eyes shut but his ears wide open. The way he holds his violin shows at once that he is a musician of the people; he is not attempting acrobatics, but simply playing a base melody to serve as accompaniment for his song. A street musician in Prague.

*H*ere I am with my people
again, with the Gypsies,
whose language I do not share
but who are so close to me that I
feel like one of them.
An identical love of music
and of the violin, an identical fire,
and often an identical history
of wandering drives us
on and pulls us together.
It is astonishing how each
of their faces tells a story:
the happiness of the man
who is clapping, the proud air
of the woman dancing
in the foreground;
the expectation and questioning
in the eyes of the child.
Yehudi Menuhin
at Amboise after a concert
with Gypsies in 1983.

The folk music tradition has always provided the cultivated and literary West with the dimensions of a primary source and a spontaneity that it lacked. Without these popular roots, the West would become a desert, a sterile kingdom which regards measure as a final purpose, uses pedantry to accommodate authority, and practices self-conscious self-control in convention. The violinist, as a child of the people, must never entirely cut its nurturing umbilical cord.

*T*he salon, once refined and removed from the rustic village, produced its own fiddling dancing masters. Armed with their violins, and with rhythm and tempo, their mission was to teach people from good society the *pas de deux*, the correct way to curtsey, and a thousand other gallantries. But to do this, they needed an elegant instrument that was easy to handle and transport—a miniature violin so small that it could be slipped into one's pocket. And so it was that the *pochette* was born. This extraordinary oblong-shaped violin, with a sound board measuring no more than eight to twelve inches long, enjoyed enormous popularity in Europe in the seventeenth and eighteenth centuries. *Pochettes* were often very elegant objects, richly inlaid with mother-of-pearl and ivory.

Even more amazing is the *Stockgeige*, or "walking-stick violin," which is nothing less than a violin so narrow that it can be kept inside a walking stick. One can imagine the shrill, rather acid tone that such an instrument would produce. But this was not important; what mattered was rhythm, the prime element of dance. Today these curiosities are the joys of private collectors and highlights at the most celebrated auctions.

*T*he *pochette*, a strange violin so small that it could be kept in a "little pocket," was the chosen instrument of the dancing masters. It was certainly not its shrill tone that made it so successful; the *pochette* was used principally for setting the rhythm for dancing. The *pochette* on the right is so refined, so richly decorated, that it must have been played only in wealthy salons. On the left is a town-house scene. The musicians are not here to teach dance, but to provide a musical decor for a romantic *tête-à-tête*. Left: Ludolf de Jongh (1616–1679), *Concert with a Pochette Player*. Aix-en-Provence, Musée Granet. Right: the astonishing nineteenth-century *pochette*.

Little by little, folk culture became civilized, and what was once rustic music became aristocratic. Village violins graced the halls of kings, street violins metamorphosed into ballroom violins, princely houses developed a taste for the rhythms of quadrilles and polkas, and Viennese salons rustled with the sound of silks swirling in waltz time.

Johann Strauss the elder—as violinist, director of balls at the Austrian court in Schönbrunn, and the "king of the waltz"—was a towering genius of what we might call the first "urban folk music," a development which has continued into the work of Leonard Bernstein and the Beatles. Better than anyone else, Strauss knew how to make Vienna dance. It was no accident that this city was for a long time the musical capital of the world, from Mozart to Mahler and Webern, via Beethoven. Placed right at the center of the map of Europe, it enriched itself with cultural influences from all directions, including even Turkish and Mongolian music.

In this vast cultural cauldron, the waltz was born, with all the power to inebriate and to tempt of the new wine made on the outskirts of Vienna. It has the scent of its forests—the Wienerwald—those same forests in which Schubert went walking and found his inspiration. It is as multilayered as the croissants which the Turks left as a memento of their passage, and as sugary as the chocolate pastries that sit so invitingly in the windows of Vienna's famous tea-shops.

Let us allow ourselves to be swept along by this intoxicating dance. The waltz is a kind of mirror that reveals the psychology and philosophy of the Viennese—a quintessential expression of the spirit and lightheartedness of the inhabitants who dance in its three-quarter time. "Glücklich ist, wer vergisst / Was doch nicht zu ändern ist" ("Happy he who forgets / what none can alter") sings Alfred in *Die Fledermaus* by Johann Strauss the younger. In other words, let's forget everything over which we have no control, let's not engage in active compassion but remain detached, philosophical and sentimental. If an innocent person ends up hanged, what can we do about it? This credo sums up the Viennese tendency to focus on the sophisticated pleasures of life. It was this same triumph of insouciance and nonchalance that led many

*A*fter a period of glory, the light, whirling, effervescent waltz went into decline. A grim demon came to beat the swinging measure of its three-quarter time. For a whole generation of Viennese who had lived in innocence and gaiety, the waltz—like the world— suddenly fell apart in 1914. World War I toppled the reassuring ramparts with which high society had surrounded itself. W. Gause, *Franz-Josef, Emperor of Austria, during the New Year's Day Ball, 1900.* Vienna, Historisches Museum der Stadt Wien.

Viennese to feel, quite innocently, that the war had given them the best years of their lives: every evening they went to concerts, opera, and balls, totally oblivious to the ongoing tragedies, trying not to think about the anti-Semitism that was forcing some of the city's finest minds into the gas chambers or exile. Paradoxically this same appetite for life produced a generosity of spirit which was so vitally important for the thousands of Hungarian refugees the Viennese welcomed to their country and into their homes during the events of 1956.

The waltz first appeared in Austria in the middle of the eighteenth century. In German *wälzen* means "to turn." The novelty of the dance lay in the fact that people danced in couples, and that they turned around themselves and around the ballroom. A veritable waltz fever gripped the princely courts of Austria and Germany, and then, during the nineteenth century, spread throughout Europe. Although it was originally a dance of the people, the waltz was danced more easily on the polished parquet floors of ballrooms than in farmyards or on the rustic floors of farmhouses.
Martin Meytens (1695–1770), *Concert for the Marriage of Joseph II and Isabel of Parma in Vienna: Serenade in the Redoutensaal.* Vienna, Schloss Schönbrunn.

*L*ike Vienna itself, the waltz is bewitching but also extremely fragile. The Viennese had become so accustomed to a life of ease and riches that they lost courage too easily. Like all civilizations that relish life to the point of an exaggerated romanticism, they go quickly from laughter to tears, from joy to melancholy, from waltz to suicide. "Lachen und weinen zu jeglicher Stunde" ("Laughing and crying at every moment"), says a Schubert song. The point of breakdown is never far away, and the waltz serves as a great fantasy, a powerful scent of flowers that opens the doors to flight and forgetting. Sometimes the edifice of frivolity and worldliness crashes down: the waltz abandons its gilded clothes and tears itself apart, as in Alban Berg's haunting violin work, the *Concerto in Memory of an Angel*. It is this richness of character—the waltz's ability to metamorphose from lightheartedness into the evocation of a darker, more bitter experience—that has made the waltz so attractive for composers from Strauss to Ravel.

I am fascinated by these complex relations between rhythm and dance, and I had the chance to explore these themes central to the Viennese soul and the original urban folk music through an unforgettable experience I had several years ago in Bath. The occasion was the final concert of my decade-long tenure of the Bath Festival, and I was appearing with my orchestra in a splendid hall that was emblematic of the spirit of unity and harmony so characteristic of this eighteenth-century city. The light from the impressive chandeliers revealed a rather unusual audience, inasmuch as everyone was dressed in period costume, appropriate for dancing; and as we went into a succession of waltzes and polkas people did indeed get up and dance. I cannot find the words to express the pleasure I experienced in seeing those people respond to my music with dance. I was the one who was making possible their movements in space. I had the feeling that I understood and was sharing what Strauss must have felt every day of his life.

THE VIOLIN: AN ANSWER TO A DREAM

Every instrument carries within itself and expresses a particular world of human dreams and imaginings. For our greater happiness, we have invented all kinds of things that fulfil our desire to organize the world of sounds: wind instruments (set vibrating in various ways through the breath), plucked stringed instruments (harp, guitar, harpsichord), bowed instruments (all the instruments in the violin family), and keyboard instruments, not to mention percussion (a category into which the piano also falls, in some respects). Within this creative profusion, we all have the chance to find the instrument that most appeals to our imagination and resonates best with our internal harmony. The violin has a particular attraction for those who play it, especially for children who choose it in preference to other instruments. Unlike the piano, which is an instrument for any purpose, commanding—through a degree of compromise—a wide range of musical expression, the violin has an individual human scale that adapts easily to a child's dimensions. It can be almost like a toy—closer even than a doll, and more alive, because it has a voice that can speak to and answer the child. And a violin can be

This charming family scene is a pastoral portrait of the young Haydn with his parents: they seem to be playing a melody of life's happiness, with the blessing of the Holy Ghost, who presides over their concert in the form of a dove. Joseph Haydn plays a *pochette*, his father the violin, and his mother the harp, while she keeps a protective and affectionate eye on her son. This drawing says much about the future composer: the importance of religion and faith, which are deeply anchored in all his work, and the happiness and serenity of his music, which had its source in a happy and harmonious childhood.
One can already hear the divine melodies and chords of his *Creation* oratorio. The Haydn family playing music: Matthias Haydn (father), Anna Maria Koller (mother), and Joseph, the eldest of twelve children. Rohrau, Austria, Joseph-Haydn-Museum.

taken up in a child's arms, cradled, and carried around in its case, which obviously would be impossible with a piano.

Furthermore, the violin is a simple instrument, at least in appearance. It is basically just a sound box plus four strings, whereas the piano has large numbers of strings controlled by a complex mechanism. The piano may perhaps appeal more readily to intellectual inclinations. The violin, on the other hand, is closer to the senses. It is an extension of the human body: it rests

on the collarbone and communicates its vibrations to our bones and the empty spaces of our bodies, which then resonate in turn. The skeleton, head, lungs, the whole of body in fact, vibrate in unison with the violin. This is one reason why certain children find the instrument so attractive—all those who are by nature close to things that breathe and vibrate, all those whose greatest satisfaction is an empathetic response to their parents, their friends, and their environment. The pianist is obliged to sit and to adapt to an immovable mass. The body is thus separated into two parts, upper and lower.

The psychological and physiological cravings of children who turn to wind instruments are quite different. Those who choose brass (the trumpet or the horn, for example) are drawn by a need to express their breathing power in different timbres of sound. Those who turn to woodwinds (such as the clarinet, oboe, or bassoon) are probably seeking a sound sensation that matches their desire for gentleness or purity

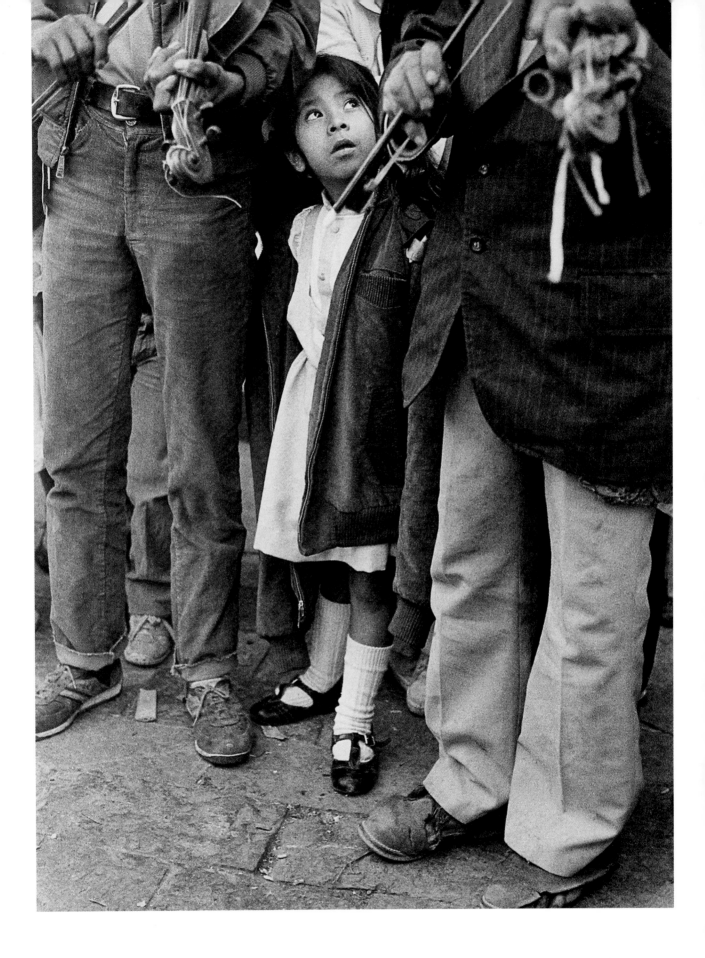

think that my instinct and need for play were completely satisfied by the violin, as if it were all toys at once.

The violin becomes both companion and another self. As I have already said, its anatomy is like that of the human body, and it soon becomes a being with whom one has to live and arrive at both understanding and agreement. We seek to persuade the violin to give its best, while at the same time expecting it to respond to our expressive requirements. Thus a dialogue and a relation of complicity are initiated.

*L*ike any close companion, the violin knows how to be a confidant. This is why it has become the preferred instrument of Jews and Gypsies, their only way of escaping from the worlds in which they lived. For Jews and Gypsies have known the same persecutions: they have both been chased and hunted because of their difference. In the imagination of our civilization, the Jew is literate, legal, imbued with the books of the Bible, the Torah and the Talmud, while the freedom-loving Gypsy is unburdened by books, furniture or possessions; but "civilized" peoples are jealous of knowledge and distrust freedom. Jews and Gypsies have expressed the same mournful song, by means of the same scale (with an augmented second). They have had to flee in the same early hours of the morning, and have, for different reasons, lived the same destiny as nomads—another attraction of the violin, which could easily be carried on their wanderings. In the course of those wanderings, they sometimes ended up sharing life in the same villages, in Romania, for example. Their continual suffering has given them an understanding of the human soul that few others can claim.

*T*his little girl will probably end up as a violinist one day. The look in her eyes speaks of her wonderment. I myself have never met a woman Gypsy violinist, but I think this situation will change: today there are many Korean and Japanese women playing violin, which would once have seemed inconceivable. In my school at Stoke d'Abernon, girls just outnumber boys. Are boys nowadays more attracted by the world of finance than by music? Musicians. Guadeloupe, Mexico, 1988.

or warmth. Percussion instruments are likely to appeal more to children with a penchant for rhythm and for the abstract and mathematical, and they correspond to an intrinsic need to respond to music's basic motive power.

It would be fair to say that the violin stands slightly apart in the world of instruments, because it can simultaneously satisfy a desire for brilliance and a desire for softness, the instincts of both high emotion and harmony, the masculine and feminine aspects of the human personality. Thanks to the richness of its sound palette and the wide range of its repertoire, the violin is several instruments rolled into one, matching several sets of human needs. I never had a real toy. I

In both cases music has become their fluent and most immediate, spontaneous expression.

I would happily yield to this spontaneity, and for that reason I have always found the image of the little Jewish musical groups characteristically portrayed by Chagall to be filled with a profound pathos.

As important as the study of great works may be, the element of improvisation conjured by these images must never be lost. So I am happy to let the Gypsies lead me away for a moment from the path of this chapter, to take a look at their fascinating history and to express some beliefs that I hold dear.

*T*he violin is an unrivaled
instrument for travel
and wandering. This is why
it has followed Jews and Gypsies
like a shadow throughout
their peregrinations.
One of the first rabbis whom
my mother met in New York
told me that when the Jews
escaping from the Russian
pogroms came as refugees
to Palestine, there was hardly one
without a violin case.
In the same way, with each wave
of Russian immigration
to present-day Israel,
a new orchestra sets up on
every street corner.
As a result, there is an impressive
concentration of violinists
in that country.

encountered en route, enriching them and also drawing from them elements which in turn have added to their identity as travelers—the history of this tireless interchange between human beings is for me a symbol of life. It is the same movement that leads from the act of giving to that of receiving, an act of love for others and love for oneself, the gesture and instinct of life. These musicians of the desert, imbued with the majesty of their environment and unashamed in their beauty and virtuosity, show us a possible road of reconciliation between people and between cultures.

Furthermore, their song, emerging from the depths of ages, can be heard in the Indian sitar, in the violin of Eastern Europe, and in the raucous, broken, passionate, and tragic voices of flamenco singers. It weaves among us a bond as indestructible as it is invisible. For all of us, at some point in history, have had to endure persecutions both great and small. We all have in common the history of a humanity which seeks its way and its voice through emotions, born of exuberance, gratitude, love, tragedy; and music is one of the most beautiful representations of that history. My foundation produced a spectacle entitled "From the Sitar to the Guitar," which attempted to recount in music and dance the epic voyage of the Gypsies. Ravi Shankar and I hosted the two evenings: it was an unforgettable experience and the audience was carried along by the superb music and dance. The Indian group found they were able to converse with the Romanian Gypsies in their traditional language, and so we could trace the binding links of culture along the routes both north and south of the Mediterranean, and to appreciate how cultures can break the barriers that human beings create.

The long journey of these people (who were also known as Bohemians, in the mistaken belief that they originated in Bohemia), their endless wanderings, from the deserts of Rajasthan to Central Europe and then to Andalusia, the way in which they have blended their cultural heritage with local traditions

*I*t is in this squatting position
that I have passed a large part
of my working life: during tours,
I often had to spend many hours
on trains. So I would close
the compartment door and wedge
my back against a cushion
for long hours of practice.
Gypsy caravans, in the days
when they were drawn by horses
on bumpy roads, would probably
not have been very suitable
for this kind of playing.
I doubt that modern caravans
are much more suitable.
Yehudi Menuhin in a Gypsy
caravan at Amboise, 1983.

An awakening of the senses and a spring-board to other places, the violin is also an instrument that demands a high degree of intuition. Every instrument requires from its performer a perfection and certain specific qualities. The violin calls for a particular kind of immediate, direct understanding that ultimately bypasses thought, as the skill becomes automatic. Intuition is crucial, because this is what enables the violinist to vibrate in resonance with the instrument.

Thus throughout a lifetime of playing, the violinist must know how to adjust the pegs of the violin in order to tune it into absolutely accurate fifths. Even before beginning to play, therefore, the violinist's instinctive awareness of the natural mathematical proportions of perfection is aroused. The apparently extraordinary phenomenon of a deaf string-player tuning his or her instrument to a perfect fifth is proof enough of the universal and overriding power of

The flamenco dancer Blanca del Rey is a miracle of a woman. She is an embodiment of centuries of determination, resistance, and survival, despite or because of the sufferings undergone by the Gypsies. For those who migrated from the East to the West, Spain represented the last hope of asylum. The Gypsies settled there, bringing with them all the way from Rajasthan the wealth of their folk music. The flamenco represents the fruit of this cross-fertilization of cultures. With Blanca, it crystallizes into the intensity of her beauty: each part of her body is just as a violin maker would have conceived it if he had sought to create a perfect body for this kind of dance. Her virtuosity and the way in which the rhythm of her feet responds to the sound of her castanets are as astonishing as the virtuosity of the Indian musicians pictured here, looking as if they have come from the pages of an Oriental storybook. "From the Sitar to the Guitar," concert, Brussels, November 1995.

discrimination between the one "right" and the many "wrongs." The pain of dissonance can be calibrated in proportion to the degree of deviation of the second note from the first, stronger note. If dissonances are small, that is "out of tune," we find it intolerable as the distance between the two notes feels like a mistake which must be corrected. If they are larger and expressive, that is melodic dissonance, *appoggiatura*, or *Vorhalte*, they must be resolved.

The string player, the wind player and the singer always communicate in perfect fifths, unlike the pianist who is keyed into "shrunken" fifths, compatible with the cycle of twelve notes which completes the chromatic scale. Curiously the tempered scale essential to the keyboard can never achieve an ideal musical therapy as the basic interval between notes is distorted.

In the absence of any reference point on the ebony fingerboard, the violinist must find the many ways of creating a fingering, a vibration. From within these tiny confines an infinity of possibilities must be created in order to arouse every kind of emotion. The violinist must be capable of carrying out all movements blind (and in some remarkable cases even deaf when his or her whole body is used to "hear.") So playing becomes not a mechanical or intellectual

The double bass was the first classical instrument to penetrate the world of jazz by means of pizzicato. The violin and its bow joined later. Jazz musicians have a true sense of rhythm, which is not the rhythm of a metronome but is dictated by emotion and an experience of life. They shape their rhythms in the same way that a sculptor works a material. Between the mechanical ticktock of the metronome and the logic of the jazz musician's inner pulse there is the same difference that exists between geometry and drawing.

undertaking, but a mobilization and sharpening of one's internal sense of hearing and musical intuition.

Furthermore, the violin, more so than any other instrument, is highly suited to the art of *rubato*, a word taken from the Italian language that literally means "stolen." *Rubato* is the art of stealing time from one note and giving it to another; you can delicately prolong a given musical moment, and then restore the stolen time later, the purpose being not to distort the overall regularity of the music's basic flow and pulse. This infinitesimal distortion in the regularity of notes gives the performance of a piece of music an undulating character, a whiff of freedom, a taste of improvisation.

A small footnote here, on the subject of organists and harpsichordists, who are often and should be great masters of the art of *rubato*. Since they are so limited by the nature of their instrument to set "stops" which once chosen allow them no control over minute differences of dynamics or timbre, the players are obliged to alter the length of the note rather than its basic timbre to achieve expression.

Needless to say, such subtlety of playing does not arise by chance; it derives from absolute control, and it has to serve the needs of the musical piece in question. The listener is generally unaware of this distortion—as if savoring a dish without being able to identify the spice that produces its specific aroma and piquancy.

This is why intuition is so essential to the violinist: it reveals what is possible—one cannot perform the same *rubatos* in the music of Bach or Beethoven as one does in a Neapolitan melody—and it helps define the exact proportions of musical style and craftsmanship. In both *rubato* and *ritardando*, it is a matter of proportion and quantity. A *ritardando*, for instance, indicates a progressive slowing of the pace, as of a wheel gradually stopping; its pace is dictated by an organic impetus in the weight of the piece as it draws to a conclusion. The dynamics and proportions between notes must depend on the phrasing and cannot be arbitrary or accidental. In general in the realm of musical interpretation, any intervention that is crude and disproportionate reduces and truncates our sensibilities. Effects can be exaggerated only during practice, but in performance they should be imperceptible, becoming so much a part of the whole concept that they can only appear as absolutely right, and never obtrusive.

VIOLINISTS

*I*n the past, the great violinists were not only performers but composers as well, playing the works
they had written: Corelli, Vivaldi, Locatelli, Geminiani,
and then, later, Paganini, Sarasate, Spohr, Wieniawski,
Vieuxtemps, Ysaÿe, Kreisler, and so forth, right through
to Joachim and Enesco. Most of the great names of the
violin were also masters in the art of composition. It
was only in the post World War II era that the composer
and the violinist yielded to a form of specialization: the
violinist became a "specialist" performer and the composer more demanding of complex detail. Fortunately
this shrinking tide is turning today as, for instance, in
my school there is more stress on creative expression, as
well as on improvisation and composition.

Today the violinist's principal task is to give life
to the works of the past, present and future; in performing, the violinist awakens the music that is locked
within the page, like the fairy-tale prince whose kiss
awakens the Sleeping Beauty, or the traveler in the Ara-
bian Nights who frees a genie trapped within a bottle.
The violinist interprets a music that was composed
decades, maybe even centuries ago, by men who left
nothing more substantial than a few signs on a score:
notes, indications of rhythm, nuance, dynamics, tempo,
mood—in short few signposts to guide the voyager
down the intricate road of musical interpretation. By
contrast, it is a particular thrill for me to have caught
the spirit of a living composer and won his approval.

This position as messenger and bearer of our
cultural heritage is simultaneously far less and far

*T*he friendship and collaboration
between Joseph Joachim
and Johannes Brahms
was indefatigable: Joachim gave
Brahms advice on the writing
of his music, which he played
in private, and on performing
it in public. The music of Brahms
is characterized by tenderness,
grandeur, and mystery.
The mystery derives from
the enchanting countryside
of his native region: his music
has the immensity and the icy
depth of the plains of the North,
wrapped in sea mists.
When he writes an *allegro*
he thinks of it as an *andante*,
his *presto* has the air
of an *allegro*; hence the sense
of dignity and nobility which
underlies his music. However,
tenderness in Brahms never
becomes sentimentality;
it is the nostalgic expression
of an all-pervading love
he felt for young people
and for the world of music.
Left: portrait of Joseph Joachim.
Right: portrait
of Johannes Brahms.
Vienna,
Society of the Friends of Music.

more onerous than the role of violinists in earlier days. For one has to know how to conjure up the emotion evoked by the composer alone and this is indeed a great responsibility! It is a matter of finding the ideal conjunction of style within the period, or the style of the composer and the personal expression with which the work is imbued. Pure emotion and the absolute integrity of style are the *sine qua non* and constant aim of the artist musician. Thus, a violinist who spends many hours working on a piece must always preserve an eternal spark of freshness. Practice or repetition are at their most effective when one is alert and can search with a clear idea of one's purpose. Practice which is merely repetitive is not only boring but numbing and unproductive. This is one of the greatest dangers for any performer.

Technique is really the elimination of the unnecessary. It is a form of housekeeping, like the dusting of corners where cobwebs gather, and it is a constant effort to avoid any possible impediment or obstacle to achieve the smooth flow of energy and intent. A violinist's "form" is not altogether a critical consideration: since, if a violinist has something really important to communicate it is often possible to overcome physical inadequacies, handicaps or imbalances, just as a messenger bringing an important letter need not be able to run perfectly. He can make a huge effort, run fast and even expire in the attempt, yet the delivery of the message will still be achieved. Playing the violin, like any art, is a combination of so many elements from the general to the particular, from the life of the individual to the fingering and phrasing, and nowhere do I feel is there an arbitrary barrier between living, playing, interpreting, and communicating.

*T*his picture is a regrettable confirmation of the fact that the tuning of a violin depends on the piano. In my opinion, it should be the piano, an instrument that is false by nature, which tunes to the violin. I have, by the way, something of a taste for out-of-tune upright pianos, which give a rustic quality and a deliciously nostalgic feel to the repertoire of peasant songs—the melodies of Grieg, for example. Listening to them, one gets the measure of the time that has passed since they were last tuned. Needless to say, such sounds would not sit well with Mozart and Schubert.

Perhaps the most important principle of "housekeeping" in violin technique is the principle of "openness," a form of neutrality which seems to obviate intruding or unbalancing elements. A useful analogy would be the way that prejudice in thought twists opinion in a particular direction and inhibits the flow of objective thought and analysis. In the same way gravity plays havoc with a violinist's phrasing: if he is not aware of the danger of the inclination to allow the weight of his arm to rest on the down bow, every down stroke will acquire an emphasis which distorts the phrase. This emphasis can be used if desired to good purpose. The importance of evenness in scales and bowing, dynamics, speed, as well as the use of many different patterns, cannot be overemphasized. But it is quite extraordinary how far the will to express oneself can overcome even minor inadequacies. Some of the greatest violinists I know have a left thumb position

One day in 1951, chance led me to the discovery of yoga. I was thumbing through a pamphlet in a waiting room. It was a brief introduction to hatha-yoga, that is, to the bodily positions, or *asanas*, and it was truly a revelation to me: I realized that here I would find the key to certain enigmas in life, as well as a means of understanding better and mastering the technique of the violin. This was the beginning of an experience that was to leave its mark on my whole life. Yoga is not only of practical usefulness. As its etymology indicates, it serves to "link together," to "unite."

In other words, it encourages a union between body and spirit, as well as a link to other people and, in its most mystical version, union with infinity and the divine. That is why this initiation can only take place under the direction of a master. Iyengar was my guru, my guide, each time I went to India, and also every summer in Europe. He is a warm, kindly person, but when it comes to yoga, he has the tenacity, determination, and demanding nature of artists of genius. For more than forty years, this discipline has helped me to establish and develop a sense of internal peace. Yehudi Menuhin and Iyengar.

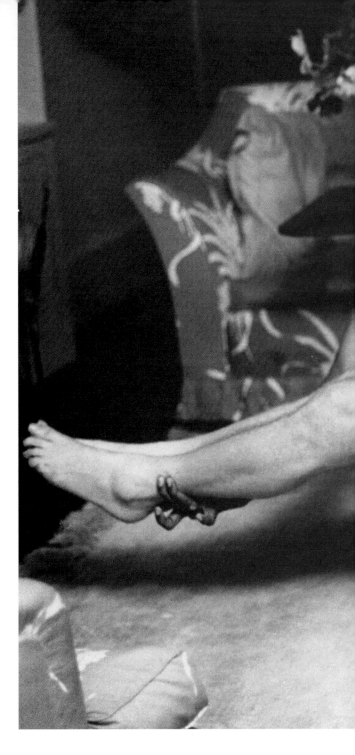

which is not absolutely ideal, but it seems irrelevant to mention this when one sees them playing and submits to the impact of their musical presence.

Relaxation and determination are equally essential to the violinist. To relax during the performance itself depends on a certain preparation: so much of our thought today is concerned with confrontation, with an assumed determination to achieve, which is not always the best condition for artistic creation or performance. Violinists have knocked their heads against tomes of Ševčik exercises only to emerge wounded and spent. A certain degree of excess strain and effort is not harmful so long as one can quickly return to a relaxed condition. It may require a few minutes of breathing

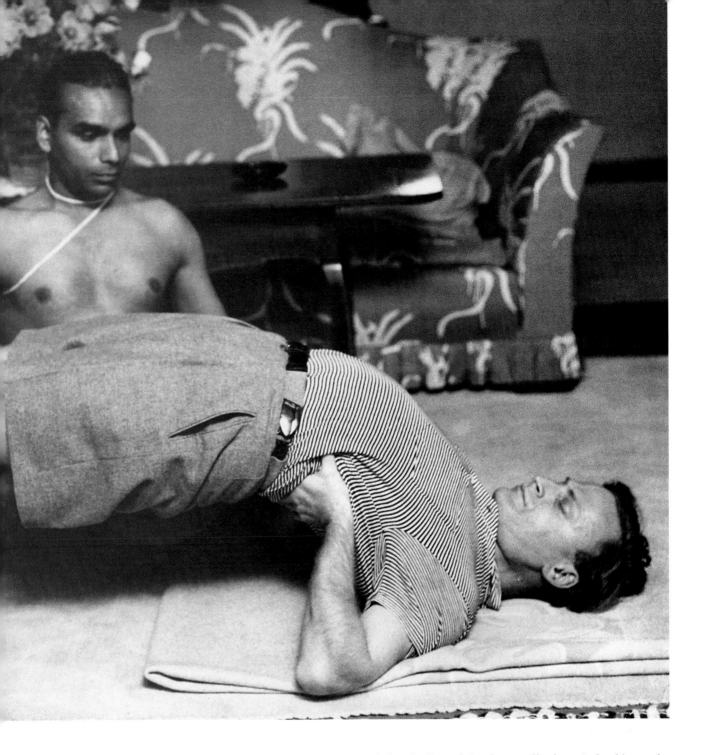

lying on the floor, a hot bath or a massage. I was lucky to be able to learn yoga whose positions and breathing exercises were most illuminating to me. To find comfort in a position without any strain, gradually yielding to the stretch, is of great benefit: the plough position, for example, (on one's back with feet behind the head, to stretch out the muscles in the legs, at the base of the skull, and in the small of one's back), or the shoulder or head stand to improve circulation. Although I have never practised T'ai Chi, it is most effective for maintaining balance in motion and I am sure various other martial arts, gymnastics, and weight-training must be extremely useful. It is a common fallacy to assume that power comes more from

*S*arasate was one of the most
highly respected violinists
of his century: in Pamplona,
his native town, one can visit
a museum that exhibits
the objects and presents
he received from sovereigns
all over the world.
This photograph reveals
a refinement worthy of a dandy.
One should remember that
in those days violinists gave far
fewer concerts than they do now:
there were no music festivals,
and without aircraft
it was difficult for a performer
to play in one capital one
evening and in another the next.
Today violinists are more like
traveling salesmen
than gentlemen such as Sarasate.
Above right: a *hardangerfele*.
This folk fiddle, inlaid with
mother-of-pearl and fitted with
strings that vibrate in resonance,
is still very common in Norway.

force than from motion, more from tension than from balance. This is an important truth to understand as it applies to violin playing in particular.

*A*mong the great names of the past, out of the multitude of virtuosi and illustrious servants of the art of the violin, I will mention three examples close to my heart because they are typical of the cultivated violinists who must always remain half folk musician, true to the nature of their instrument and preserving the vital links that united them to their people—to their land and to their dance.

Pablo de Sarasate (1844–1908), a Basque composer, was a native of Pamplona. He gave his first concert at the age of seven; then he left for the Paris Conservatoire, where he studied with Delphin Alard. His technique was dazzling, his playing the height of elegance, and the greatest composers of the nineteenth century competed for him to play their works. Lalo wrote his brilliant *Symphonie espagnole* for Sarasate, as well as his *Concerto in F*; it was for him that Saint-Saëns composed his *Concerto in B Minor* and the *Introduction and Rondo Capriccioso in A Minor*; Max Bruch offered his *Scottish Fantasy* to him. Sarasate was famed throughout the world, and he toured Europe, North and South America, and the East.

The wealth of Spanish musical idiom, the many dances which have absorbed Gypsy, African and Arab influences, inspired Sarasate to compose works in the popular style, works which remain among the most moving and affective violin pieces ever written. His collections of *Spanish Dances* have the charm, piquancy, and passion of the music he had heard as a child in the streets and cafés of his native land. Before

Albéniz, Falla, Granados among others, Sarasate had found a way to give a voice to the land in which he was born. Although a great master and universally appreciated for his interpretations of the major classical repertoire, his fire came from Spain's popular traditions. He fused the music we nowadays call classical with the music of his people.

Ole Bull's (1810–1880) inspiration came from the traditional Norwegian *hardangerfele*, the "hardanger fiddle," an instrument with four stopped strings and four resounding ones which provide the drones against which the melody is played, as in the Scottish bagpipes. It is a folk instrument invented in the middle of the seventeenth century, and it was originally used to accompany the recitations of bards. Bull had studied the playing of this astonishing instrument with Norwegian peasants and even went so far as to adapt his own violin, an Amati, so that he could play his country's folk music.

This Norwegian musician enjoyed extraordinary fame in Europe and America. In London he joined Liszt in playing Beethoven's *Kreutzer Sonata*. Audiences appreciated the warmth and verve of his playing, and Ole Bull took advantage of their admiration to make the music, the songs and dances of his country known to a wider public. He was also a fine conductor.

Bull composed many pieces stamped with that mixture of nostalgia and raw danger so characteristic of Norwegian mythology and folklore. His works are not exceptional, but he was Norway's great patriotic violinist. Following Ole Bull, and directly thanks to him—since it had been Bull who discovered his talent and persuaded his parents to send him to Leipzig—Edvard Grieg composed the music so deeply moving, so beloved of his people. With Grieg, Bull opened the way for a celebration of the origins and heritage of his country.

Finally, Joseph Joachim (1831–1907) arranged nearly fifty Hungarian dances which Brahms had composed on the basis of the Hungarian idiom with its incredibly rich range of emotion. Bartók too has bequeathed us a violin based on Eastern European and Turkish motifs. Among the first works I played was the *Symphonie Espagnole* by Édouard Lalo, a work which allowed my imagination to cast me in a Spanish role: at the time I knew hardly anything about Spain, but the music conveyed its images, character, and rhythms. I always felt at home with Spanish music as

*O*le Bull and Edvard Grieg are the two representatives of Norwegian music. As a self-taught violinist of genius, Bull traveled the world in a series of triumphal tours and created a Norwegian national music by drawing inspiration from his country's folk music: the dances, ballads, and songs of the shepherds. Ole Bull in Berlin in 1877.

*G*rieg continued Ole Bull's
project by composing works
in a language that was both
popular and universal, particularly
in the realm of song.
I was once playing some
of Grieg's works in a concert
before an audience of Norwegians,
when I realized that they were
all in tears. It is the very fabric
of their identity which has
been transfigured in this music.
Franz von Lembach,
Portrait of Edvard Grieg.
Bergen, Norway, Grieg House.

*F*ritz Kreisler and Jacques Thibaud each in their own way embodied elegance and musical refinement. When I was a child, Kreisler fascinated me because his was the language of a world that was foreign to me—that of Viennese society life. I knew the spirit of the Russians, the Germans, and the French, but Viennese culture was totally outside my experience. Kreisler played his arrangements of Viennese tunes with a brilliance that I found impossible to imitate. I could reproduce all styles except his. I had to wait till the age of twenty before recording the *Schön Rosmarin* and the *Caprice Viennois*. As for Thibaud, I shall never forget the Mozart *Concerto in G Major* he played at the Gaveau concert hall in Paris in the early 1930s. We later became very close. In life, as on the concert platform, he was most courteous, elegant, and amusing, a ladies' man to perfection. Left: Fritz Kreisler with Yehudi Menuhin. Right: portrait of Jacques Thibaud by Abel Faivre.

indeed with so many other folk idioms. Thus the violin helped me to bridge the world between the popular fiddle and the great works of the musical repertoire.

*E*ach culture has produced its composers—some have gone beyond the dimensions of the folk pieces to give us works of enormous breadth and originality—others have remained more closely in touch with their folk traditions, such as Grieg in Norway, Copland in the United States, Glinka, and Rimsky-Korsakov in Russia. As a boy I was particularly attracted to Fritz Kreisler (1875–1962) who brought the urban folk idiom of Vienna to my young ears in San Francisco, a world far as far removed from my own personal experience as Indian music. Kreisler's work, however, belonged to the ambiance of Mozart, Haydn and Beethoven with whose works I was already familiar. His Viennese arrangements attracted me greatly, all the more so as I could not find the proper lilt, which evaded me for some years until 1935 when, to my delight, I was finally able to recorded his *Schön Rosmarin*. Alongside Kreisler I particularly admired Jacques Thibaud (1880–1953), the great French violinist, for his elegance and grace: his name is perpetuated through the Jacques Thibaud competition which I often direct in Paris. I remember Thibaud's performance of the Mozart D Major Number 4, a melting slow movement and a dancing last movement which could never be surpassed.

One of the most prolific generations of violinists came to Western Europe and the United States as a result of the Russian Revolution and the tragic fate of many Jewish people in Russia. At the Odessa Conservatory, in Moscow and to an important degree in major

*D*avid Oistrakh was
the most complete violinist
of our age: he combined
a passionate fervor with
an absolute rigor and control.
His extraordinary
artistic personality went hand
in hand with an exceptional
honesty, warmth, and generosity.
As a Russian Jew, originally from
Odessa, he even remained loyal
to his country: he could have
pursued his career anywhere
in the world, but he chose
to stay faithful to the USSR.
No colleague has ever been closer
to me; until his premature death,
he was a priceless friend.
It was thanks to him that I
was able to play,
and to introduce to the West,
Shostakovich's *Violin Concerto*
(it had been written for him,
and he had given me the score),
as well as the Prokofiev *Sonata*.
A fine example of
the selflessness and magnanimity
that were his hallmark!
From left to right:
Yehudi Menuhin, Ravi Shankar,
David Oistrakh.

centers like Kiev and St Petersburg one could find great violin teachers, and perhaps the most famous of them was Leopold Auer. From his stable alone emerged Jascha Heifetz, Misha Elman, Tosha Seidel and many others. These violinists achieved a degree of intensity, expression and performance technique not seen on that scale since the days of Paganini. These were not composers but rather single-minded virtuosi who knew they had the gifts to conquer the world. Heifetz came directly across the Pacific, others came with Auer first to Europe, stopping in Norway and then traveling on to New York. As a boy of ten I visited

Ginette Neveu was the first among the great women violinists. I have rarely known an artist more devoted to her instrument: she was capable of working day and night. A pupil of Enesco and Carl Flesch, she was a very powerful personality, whose playing was relaxed but at the same time had an authority and a force worthy of an Ysaÿe. There were many other women violinists, including the graceful Cecilia Hansen, but their playing was transparent and delicate, whereas Ginette Neveu belonged to the race of passionate performers, burning with a volcanic fire.

Carnegie Hall in New York and I have a vivid memory of seeing Auer who was wearing a skullcap.

Perhaps it was because all the ingredients necessary for the magic, the comprehension, and the teaching of the violin were united in this one region. The Ukraine was an intense cultural melting pot: the violin playing of the Gypsies brought instinct and fire, which served as a kind of raw material. Then there were the Jews, who allied emotion to an innate gift for analyzing, dissecting, and reconstructing matter and concepts—which is why the teaching of music took root and flourished. And as a final contribution, the Ukrainian peasants offered their natural penchant for drama and heightened sentiment.

Furthermore, in this harsh and sometimes hostile world, the violin was the only means of escape. The life of these people was miserable; as my wife so rightly says, it was spent between the mud of summer and the snows of winter. This was also the lot of all the inhabitants of old Russia. For the Ukrainians, playing the violin was the only way of forgetting their distress, their only way of exorcising it. Rather like the situation in Italy at the moment when Amati's violin was born, there was in the Ukraine a conjunction of all the elements propitious to the emergence of a Russian school, as bright as summer sunshine and as fiery as a stallion on the high plains. The ear and the temperament of the students and teachers who lived there were somehow conditioned and predestined to the incendiary music of the violin. The Russian school continued to provide some of the greatest violinists we know: for example David Oistrakh and Dmitri Sitkovetsky, and it continues in Israel particularly to bring forth great violinists, Itzhak Perlman being perhaps the most famous. But in the last 50 years we have seen the arrival of similar waves from Asia, Japan, Korea, South-East Asia, Singapore, Malaysia and increasingly from China. These musicians pursue the classical canon of Western music with a dedication, devotion, adoration, and love which is truly overwhelming.

Among hitherto neglected groups of musicians, women too are playing the violin in increasing numbers. Our music schools and orchestras are beginning to have a majority of women who are achieving heights of playing which, as one might expect, establish the very highest standards. The great American violinist Maud Powell (1868–1920), who just overlapped with me, was world renowned. She began her career brilliantly in Berlin and also worked in France with Charles Dancla. She won the hearts of audiences in both Europe and America. As well as forming her own quartet she also left several compositions for the violin. There was also the English violinist Isolde Menges, and the Russian-trained Cecilia Hansen whom I loved to hear playing in San Francisco when I was a boy. In her white dress she appeared to me as an angel who played with great beauty. One of the greatest of women violinists was Ginette Neveu, whose tragic death in an airplane accident was a grievous loss to the world and to France in particular. I would also mention Anna Chumachenko who many years ago won a high prize in the Brussels concours (named for the late Queen Elizabeth of the Belgians). Her simple explanation of how she preserved her serenity while she waited to play as the last of ten, was typically modest: "I've always dreamed of playing a Beethoven concerto with orchestra." She remains a wonderful chamber player, violinist, and teacher.

Younger contemporary women violinists who have reached the heights are Anne-Sophie Mutter and a few decades ago, the Italian, Gioconda da Vita. There are of course many more, but henceforth I feel that we should make no differentiation between the sexes as we shall have as many great women violinists as men. Incidentally, in the field of conducting there are also extraordinary women artists. It is of course a sight not likely to be found as yet in Islamic countries, but I hope and pray it will be not long in coming.

And what about the orchestral violinists! Shadowy figures, but at the same time figures of light, these violinists have still not won the recognition they deserve. Sitting in serried rows, often hidden by their music stands, they work to create a common sound quality, so that the audience hears only a single voice and sees only the elegant ballet of their graceful bows, moving as if by clockwork. This musician, however, albeit a nameless face for the audience, must often have qualities greater than those of a soloist, particularly if playing the first violin. He or she must be capable of following and responding to the conductor's indications and sufficiently flexible to adapt to all repertoires, because, unlike soloists, who often build their careers on the basis of a fixed and limited repertoire, the orchestral musician is obliged to decipher and play the many different works required by the season's program. This same musician must also be able to play the solo phrase, a theme, or an entire passage, as occasion demands. Fortunately, professionals and music lovers are becoming increasingly aware of the talent of these musicians, but this recognition has been so long in coming that there is no harm in rendering homage once again.

*I*n the collectivity of an orchestra it is important that everyone has their place and receives the recognition they deserve. One often forgets these artists of the shadowy world, whose faces are not even visible in this photograph, and who in the most sophisticated of today's symphonic arrangements (as here the Vienna Philharmonia) cannot work without stands or electric lighting. However it is through the dedication and the talent of each one of these musicians that the conductor can elicit a beauty and emotional power from the whole orchestra.

There are a few violinists who are already exemplars for the violinists of tomorrow. Gilles Apap, and two from my own school, Nigel Kennedy and Volker Biesenbender, who bridge the worlds of classical, jazz and traditional music. They know the folk music from the Amazon to the sacred city of Benares. I was very happy to learn that Volker had set up a small group, with violin, accordion, and bass, like those one finds in Chagall's pictures, and that the three of them were playing in the streets of Basel with great success. Biesenbender came to give a promenade concert at the Gstaad Festival, and the audience followed him around as if he were the Pied Piper of Hamelin.

Another of my pupils, Nigel Kennedy, also bridges several worlds. He was in a sense liberated when Stéphane Grappelli came to visit my school. Nigel developed a boundless admiration for Grappelli, who took him under his wing and guided him on his way. One of the most wonderful young violinists is the Frenchman Gilles Apap who can play Irish jigs as well as Indian and Gypsy music, and is also familiar with the classics.

Today the violinist virtuoso must know more than a few solo concerti, not merely a sonata, but must be a chamber music player as Joachim, Ysaÿe, and Enesco have been. The violinist must have a flair for and interest in musics that are no longer strange— Indian, African, Balinese, Chinese and the folk music of South America and Mexico. He or she will also be inclined to improvise and to compose. The great orchestral conductor Bruno Walter used to say of the repertoire that he conducted: "If only I could hear these works for the first time!" It seems to me that the pursuit of composition and improvisation will help us rediscover the original thrill and the untouched freshness of these works of the past. And thus the great spiral of creativity from the age of Corelli and Vivaldi, the profusion of Italian composers and violinists, will continue reaching up to ever higher levels.

This mosaic of Plato
and his disciples, serenely
meditative and listening
attentively, is an eloquent
illustration of what the teaching
of music can be.
People imagine that teachers
simply imprint things
on to their students,
as if they were just raw material
in the hands of a sculptor.
But it is the music itself
that transforms the person
who studies it. The situation
is analogous to that of the sower,
who has very little influence on
the seed he sows: he can prepare
the soil, decide the propitious
moment for planting, but
afterwards has no control over
the actual growth of the seed.
In the same way, the music
teacher sets a process in motion,
rather than imposing it.
The Assembly of Wise Men,
or *School of Philosophers,*
Plato and His Disciples, mosaic.
Naples,
Museo Archeologico Nazionale.
Edme Bouchardon (1698–1762),
Les Semeurs.
Paris, Musée du Louvre,
Cabinet des Dessins.

THE VIOLIN TEACHER

*T*he ability to teach is a gift: a gift of experience, an amalgam of mistakes and discoveries, successes and failures; a gift as unpredictable as the seed the farmer sows, not knowing whether or not it will germinate, which becomes a plant in its own right and produces a new seed, thus completing the great cycle of nature and creation.

The teaching process ripens over time. The teacher has to accompany the student along the road of learning, channeling the student's energies, listening and guiding. But, above all, the teacher's role is to instruct the student in the art of self-correction, of analyzing, and of thinking, taking decisions, then applying them to the task at hand. The teacher's ultimate aim is for the student to become independent—to become a master rather than a pupil, while the teacher must be both.

THE GREAT TEACHERS AND THEIR METHODS

*A*ll teachers must have an ability to listen, to watch, and to be sensitive to the personalities of their students. If a teacher notices a defect in a student, merely pointing it out is not sufficient. Anyone can see and criticize other people's mistakes; rather, the teacher must search for the basic cause and get to the root of the problem. For example, if one plays the violin with a poor sense of rhythm, the teacher should observe how the pupil walks or dances. Improper playing may be the result of a physical or technical shortcoming rather than a student's unwillingness to learn. Only teaching consituted of patience and imagination can give the pupil the drive and the spirit that are so necessary for the harmonious development of talent and personality.

*O*ne of the first great teachers in the history of the violin was Leopold Mozart, father of Wolfgang Amadeus. His book on violin method, published in 1756 (*Versuch einer gründliche Violinschule*, or *Essay on the Fundamental Principles of Violin Technique*) quickly became the standard reference work. The book analyzes what was then the thorny question of the finger position on the fingerboard, along with ways of holding the instrument, and bowing technique.

You can be sure that Mozart would never have become a composer without the presence of his father as teacher. It was Leopold Mozart who listened to his son's first attempts at music and guided his first steps. In this portrait, Leopold displays with perhaps a touch of arrogance, that tranquil sense of self-confidence characteristic of people who are in control of their craft. There is no doubt that he was the right person to help Wolfgang Amadeus' talent blossom. His hand rests on a book, probably his famous volume on violin method, which introduced the Germans to the artistic principles of the Italian virtuosi. Today this work is still used by violinists, for it provides precious information about *appoggiature* and ornamentation in the eighteenth century. Pietro Antonio Lorenzoni or Augsburg F. J. Degle, *Portrait of Leopold Mozart*. Salzburg, Mozart-Museum.

Violin techniques today have changed considerably, but the writings of Leopold Mozart are still highly respected, because they are a mine of information, particularly concerning ornamentation and the kinds of *appoggiature* that were played by the artists of the time.

I am not going to present a long list of all the great teachers the West has produced, but I would like to recall a few names and consider a few developments.

*A*round 1800, the violin became incredibly popular, thanks in particular to virtuosi such as Paganini. The more the public became interested in the violin, the more composers wrote for it, and the more musicians began to play it. As a result, the number of teachers increased. Some of them composed pieces that were vital elements in the pedagogy of the violin, as for example, the French violinist Rodolphe Kreutzer, with his *Études* and *Caprices for Solo Violin*. Together with Rode and Baillot, Kreutzer founded the modern French school of violin playing.

Violin teaching and playing moved from Italy to France, Germany, and Austria. In each capital city the conservatoire produced violinists of great style, who belonged to a recognizable school. Thus all the great Italians beginning with Corelli, Vivaldi, Locatelli, Tartini up to Paganini gave birth to a French school marked by Pierre Baillot (1771–1842), Rodolphe Kreutzer (1766–1831), the dedicatee of Beethoven's famous sonata, and Pierre Rode (1744–1830). The bridge between Italy and France was Giovanni Battista Viotti (1775–1824) who like Paganini traveled a lot and

Leopold Auer is one of the most impressive figures in the history of violin teaching. This Hungarian Jew, who emigrated to Russia, was the teacher of Heifetz, Elman, Zimbalist, Seidel, and Milstein. When he left Russia for New York—passing through Norway, he stayed for a while in Oslo—he took his pupils with him, except Heifetz, who later arrived from the West over the Pacific. I heard Heifetz at his first concert in America in San Francisco, when I was seven.

Unlike many teachers, Auer has left us no studies or exercises, but he is the author of a small practical book of method which I read when I was very young.

was a favorite in London. The Belgian branch of the French school of violin playing also derived from Viotti, through the intermediary of Charles Auguste de Bériot (1802–1870).

There was however another school which came from Russia and the Slavic countries and which represented the conquering of a less cultivated and more spontaneous, earthy violin style. The great Hungarian teacher responsible for his famous Ukrainian disciples such as Heifetz, Milstein, Zimbalist, Elman and Seidl, was Leopold Auer (1845–1930).

Auer owed much of his method to the German school having been a pupil of Joachim and Dont. He was finally appointed in his native St. Petersburg as successor to Henryk Wieniawski. There he taught for almost fifty years, having redirected a performing career as a virtuoso into a teaching career. He must have been a formidable performer as his recordings even at the age of eighty were more controlled than those of his pupils when they were much younger. Tchaikovsky, who was an admirer, dedicated his great violin concerto to Auer. The first performance was given by Adolf Brodsky, possibly a pupil of Auer, while Auer himself often played the concerto on later occasions. After the Russian Revolution, Auer emigrated to New York.

Another great Jewish Hungarian teacher, Carl Flesch (1873–1944), who taught Ida Haendel, Ginette Neveu, and many others, left us an autobiography and also a precious teaching text, *The Art of Playing the Violin*, which was published in Berlin in 1923 and contains a whole series of methodical scales and arpeggios. The exercises he recommends for the violinist's morning warm-up are particularly well designed. Carl Flesch lived in London during World War II. The City of London violin competition bore his name until it was discontinued.

It is remarkable that Hungary was so fertile in producing great teachers. The reason must lie in the country's historical interweaving of East and West and the presence of diverse musical traditions, including that of the Gypsies and Hungarian folk music.

In the nineteenth century, Hungary had already made its contribution to violin teaching in the person of Joseph Joachim (1831–1907). Having settled in

*T*chaikovsky, the composer who has given violinists the most anguish, because no violinist, particularly a Russian, has ever foregone the ambition to play his *Concerto in D*, and all have spent useless hours practising it. I must be the only one never to have recorded it—at least not deliberately: although I played it often as a boy the only two extant recordings of my performances are pirated. Through his genius, Tchaikovsky expressed the soul of the Russian people, with all its paradoxes and contrasts. What people often highlight in his music is mainly its grandiose, dramatic aspect. However, the delicacy and "balletic" quality of his compositions are at least equally important.

N. Kuznetsov,
Portrait of Peter Ilich Tchaikovsky.
Moscow, Tretyakov Gallery.

Another legendary figure
in the history of the violin,
Joseph Joachim, was a wonderful
violinist, an eminent teacher,
and a composer and conductor.
He was one of the most
famous and honored violinists
of his century. Here we see
another facet of his incredible
musical vitality: in 1869,
in Berlin, he founded a quartet,
the Joachim Quartet,
with which he was to play until
the end of his life, interpreting
the Beethoven quartets
in particular. Looking
at these serious people,
dressed in their orthodox
German dignity, it is a surprise
to see the unorthodox
seating order.
We see, from left to right,
Joseph Joachim (first violin),
Roberto Hausmann (cello),
Emmanuel Wirth (viola),
and Karl Halir (second violin).

Germany, Joachim had fired the enthusiasm of Mendelssohn and Liszt. He was the founder of a quartet which championed the Beethoven quartets. Both Schumann and Brahms sought his advice when writing their works for violin. Joachim was Auer's teacher in Hanover, but he also taught Jenó Hubay, Willy Hess, and, briefly, Bronislaw Huberman. His influence during the second half of the nineteenth century is immense. To today's violinists, he has bequeathed a voluminous book of violin method, as well as cadenzas for the Beethoven and Brahms concertos that are still highly respected.

In this constellation of great teachers, there is, for instance, the Czech violinist Otakar Ševčik (1832–1914), who taught at the Prague Conservatory, and to whom aspiring violinists would flock from all over the world. He was nicknamed the "executioner of violinists": few of his students went on to careers as violinists, since few survived his drill, the exercises taking up the greater part of the day. They were "killed" by an excess of uninspired technique. While discipline and precision are necessary, they should never stifle expression nor the individual's temperament, lest they become counter-productive, transforming the original dynamic drive of a student into something destructive and infinitely boring. Technique is born of the music it serves, and by severing technique from music we are reducing both. In the same way that the flame of a candle needs not only the wick but oxygen as well to keep burning, so the violinist cannot play without the emotion that swells both the spirit and the lungs. No violinist is merely a machine for producing notes, but a being of flesh and blood, a sublimation of desires and passions.

*I*n teaching, there are no fixed, eternal answers. One is always looking for new approaches, a way of explaining things that matches the pupil's personality, or a composer's specific style, or the character of a work. This is perhaps why, in this photograph, I have such a studious look: the right musical solution can only be arrived at as a result of careful thought. There is always so much to say about any given work; one can always find a better way to make the very marrow of a piece vibrate. The young viola player in this picture, Paul Coletti, is working on the Brahms *Viola Sonata*. Yehudi Menuhin with a student at the Gstaad International Academy of Music, August 1980.

*S*uzuki has done much to popularize the teaching of violin by giving it an element of play. In his method, the child learns the violin while walking about and playing at the same time. Suzuki broke through what had been an extremely static way of teaching, sometimes based too much on constraint. His ambition was to train thousands of amateurs. The wish is realized here, on the occasion of his yearly violin gathering, where three thousand children stand in a circle to play Bach's *Double Violin Concerto*.

It is possible to stretch a pupil's capacity: this added expectation—not least by the pupil of himself—is beneficial, so long as it does no permanent damage. One should be careful not to exceed certain limits, a caution sports' trainers know well.

*A*t the end of the nineteenth century, France and Belgium reached particular heights in the personalities of Charles de Bériot, Henri Vieux-temps (1820–1881), and his pupil, Eugène Ysaÿe (1858–1931).

Ysaÿe was uncontestably the dominant figure in this school, one of the last superstars of a bygone era: a colossus in physical presence as in the sweep of his bow and the power of his conception. Many composers were inspired by his playing and dedicated works to him: Chausson's *Poème*, the César Franck and Guillaume Lekeu *Sonatas*, and the Debussy *Quartet*. He saw himself as working within a tradition, a tradition he wanted to transmit.

Ysaÿe was an excellent composer himself and has bequeathed to us among other works six *Violin*

Concertos and six brilliant *Sonatas for Solo Violin.* My first teacher, Louis Persinger, had studied with Ysaÿe and I met the great man himself, who was in a sense my musical "grandfather," in Brussels in 1927.

At the turn of the century there continued to be excellent French violin teachers: Charles Dancla (1817–1907) and, until only a quarter of a century ago, Jules Boucherit (1878–1962). Their refinement and their musical sense enabled them to maintain an ideal balance between method and inspiration.

*T*he violin has seized the imagination of the Asian peoples just as it became the favorite stringed instrument in India two hundred years ago. It has now conquered vast territories in Asia.

Perhaps the most famous teacher today is Shin'ichi Suzuki, a genial Japanese who was determined to make the early stages of violin playing into a game for children—a very worthy ambition. He felt the spark must never be extinguished and set himself up with this intention, hoping to create in his own words "thousands of amateurs." He valued the

*T*o play in a chamber orchestra,

to appear before an audience,

to meet musicians from other

countries, these are all crucial

steps in a musical apprenticeship.

They are some of the elements

I attempt to provide

for the young string

instrumentalists who participate

in my International Academy

of Music at Gstaad.

They come from the four corners

of the world to exchange

different points of view

and compare different

approaches to music.

Although most of them are

already very advanced,

they find in this academy

a precious adjunct to

their musical formation.

amateur violin player as much as the professional, and in this case he was absolutely right.

The teaching is completely by imitation, partly individual and more importantly by group. Suzuki encourages parents, especially one, to be present, and if qualified to continue instruction at home between lessons. This approach has kindled groups all around the world; there is hardly a city that does not have a Suzuki trained teacher.

While it may have a few drawbacks in matters of technique, repertoire, and a ritual aspect which probably seems exaggerated for Western tastes, Suzuki's approach is sympathetic and endearing. Certainly he is on the right road, and moreover he realizes that one does not construct high towers without a broad base.

I long nurtured the idea of a music-teaching boarding school. Some thirty years ago, I set up my own school in England. Just like Suzuki I wanted to spare children the ordeal of poor teaching yet at the same time I wanted to produce players and human beings at the highest levels. My first school at Stoke d'Abernon in Surrey, England, was inspired by the Central School in Moscow which I had seen on my first trip there in 1945. We have, naturally, British children, but also children from Europe, Asia, the Americas, and hopefully soon from Africa. They find at the school teachers for all the stringed instruments, including the double bass and very importantly the piano, and all elements for a general education at which the children excell. These children are highly motivated and have a great capacity for both the raw materials of living experience and the finished material of excellence in their chosen profession.

Beyond conveying these principles, our role is to provide the children with high-quality teachers, time to practice, the opportunities to play in public and work with other children, as well as access to other courses of study and musical activities—for example improvisation or the art of composition. In this way, their artistic gifts can blossom, like a bud that opens and metamorphoses first into a flower and then into a fruit. Our objective is partly to train excellent musicians, but also to develop people who are open, well balanced, and ready to contribute to a universal harmony among people.

*T*he spike of the cello roots the instrument in the ground. This is also true in musical terms, because it is the cello that plays the lowest line of a string quartet. The cellist is therefore often the most "musical" figure in the quartet, providing the basis of the harmony and supporting the whole musical edifice. When a young musician chooses the cello, it often indicates a particular temperament. While violins need simply a fine voice and a passionate character, rather like tenors or prima donnas, the cello demands a depth, a tranquility, and an unusual degree of seriousness.

All my life I have had the privilege of knowing and of playing with the world's greatest cellists such as Pablo Casals and Mstislav Rostropovich. Casals had a jeweler's precision and eye for detail, while still speaking a profound language of emotion. Rostropovich is relaxed, free and impulsive, but nonetheless disciplined down to the last demisemiquaver. These two giants, on a par with each other, brought to life, through the passion of their playing, the most beautiful qualities that music has ever produced.

PLAYING THE VIOLIN

*T*he violin and its deep-voiced brother, the viola, are the only stringed instruments supported by the body and held by the arms. The cello stands on its spike and rests on the ground, the cellist being seated; the double bass is also in direct contact with the ground. But the violin and the viola rest against and upon the body of the player.

This is why the first reflex of the child, who is naturally scared of dropping both violin and bow, is to hold the violin clamped in a tight grip between

*W*hen the violin rests on the shoulder (photo, left) and not, as it should, on the collarbone, the effect compromises the ideal stance— the left arm is reduced in freedom and very stifled. The shoulder should remain low and relaxed (photo, right), whatever the position of the left hand.

When the muscles of the shoulder are tense, the muscular circuit that goes from the back to the left hand is interrupted; equilibrium and freedom of movement are thus reduced. An example of correct and incorrect ways of holding the violin, as demonstrated by Bruno Monsaingeon.

shoulder and chin, a position which immediately restricts the performance. However inhibiting this position, teachers still ask students to rest and hold the violin on their shoulder, which causes the raising of the shoulder, the twisting of the neck and head, and the clamping of the violin between chin or jaw and shoulder. These teachers have forgotten the role of the collarbone which is an ideal resting place for the violin, enhancing the vibration of the spaces below the bone, permitting the left arm its freedom to swing, and allowing the vibration of the fingers to take place without tightening the grip between thumb and fingers. The shoulder must remain free. I have designed exercises which aim to separate the collarbone from the left shoulder and to give the left arm and the shoulder full freedom. The shoulder rest which has come into prominence in my lifetime only (previously one used only cloth pads) is now often of a height which keeps the head unnaturally tilted back and inhibits the movement of the left arm and the fingers. In fact, the shoulder should be able to float and move in different directions, compensating for the changing positions of the arm as they are dictated by the hand's movements on the fingerboard.

Gravity and weight, momentum and continuity of motion are at the very heart of violin playing. The balance of the body even without the violin, from the very toes and heels, the arch of the feet, the spread of the toes, and the head delicately poised brushing the chinrest—these require dynamic adjustments which are constantly in flux and balance as the body creates different proportions of gravity and momentum.

The left thumb and fingers should be complementary to one another. The violin should be free to

*O*ne would love to be able to play the violin with such grace, such nonchalance, such dreamy relaxation. Unfortunately, the vision here is slightly idealized. The angle of the elbow is perfect, but the position of the fingers on the bow is unrealistic; it would be impossible to play like this. Giovanni Bellini (c. 1430–1516), *San Giobbe Altarpiece* (detail, 1486–87). Venice, Gallerie dell'Accademia.

be rolled between the thumb and any finger of the left hand. This happens if the violin is left to roll by the chin; if it is gripped too hard no amount of finger movement can roll it.

The same principles of suppleness and flexibility apply to the bow. As with a vibrating string which instantly stops when touched, the bow must be allowed to vibrate on the string as far as possible, carrying a minimum of weight and held as softly as possible, almost at the very point of dropping, with the fingers flexible. It is the bow which maintains the string in a constant state of vibration. Each finger has its own function but together they balance the weight of the bow in whatever position the arm is found.

With beginners it is better to start holding and playing the violin in the second position. The hand is thus free of the body of the violin and the arm not too stretched out, remaining where the violin is lighter. This is far better than proceeding in a blind bureaucratic way from first to fifth positions, skipping second and fourth in a nonsensical fashion. As soon as possible I would encourage the child to slide up and down at different speeds and on different lengths of string. This ensures that the left arm is free and never rigidly bound down.

THE MUSICIAN AS ENCHANTER

I never really had a violin teacher as such: I had only great musicians who happened to be great teachers as well. They served as an example and are responsible for the richness of my musical life at present. They all played like angels and did not want to impose a method on a child with notable ability.

*T*his teacher is in the process of adjusting the position of the young student's left hand. This is one of the delicate points of violin technique: in general, the position of the right hand, which holds the bow, is better taught by teachers, even though the thumb remains a hidden element. The way in which the violin is held with the left hand is fundamental, because, just as you can stop the vibrations of a bell or a glass by a touch of the hand, so a poor holding position can hinder the violin's freedom of vibration. The hand, moreover, is not isolated from other parts of the body. Incorrect playing with the left hand is often the result of a bad shoulder position. However, as usual, the tendency is to correct only symptoms, to correct only the things one sees.

Louis Persinger, who had studied with Ysaÿe, was the first. He played first violin in the San Francisco Symphony Orchestra, and inspired me with his two rare violin solos, as in *Sheherazade* by Rimsky-Korsakoff. I had had my eye on him since I was three, when my parents took me to the weekly afternoon concerts at the Curran Theater, long before there was a concert hall in San Francisco.

I began working with him when I was six, and I shall never forget the first lesson, when instead of asking me to play, he chose to perform for my mother and me the *adagio* from Bach's *Sonata in G minor for Solo Violin*. We sat transfixed and at the end of the "lesson" we walked out on to the street and knew exactly what I wanted to become.

Persinger did not explain things to me: he played. I did not try to understand: I imitated. We let things fall into place naturally. My fingerings and the positions of my hand were guided by my ear and my instinct. Like many other teachers, Persinger could

A violin player should
never lose the sensation
of fluidity, suppleness, balance,
and gentleness.
Even in the most active phases,
freedom of impulse and flow
of energy is the rule.
Yehudi Menuhin giving a lesson
to a pupil at his school at Stoke
d'Abernon, September 1965.

have stifled the living matter that was surging up in me through hours of sterile, mechanical scales. He could, with the best of all possible intentions, have imposed on me a method that was arbitrary and wretched.

But he never did. He knew exactly what I needed, even to the extent of writing down in his meticulous musical handwriting a series of scales in thirds in all keys—but he gave up when he saw that I had no stomach for that kind of exercise!

He finally decided that I should continue with the man who had been his teacher—Eugène Ysaÿe. We crossed the Atlantic on the *De Grasse* in 1926, and then traveled via Le Havre and Paris, where we settled at 96 rue de Sèvres. I was ten years old when I knocked on Ysaÿe's door in Brussels, accompanied by my mother.

I was expecting to meet a giant. In fact, I found a wounded oak tree, for by then Ysaÿe was past his prime and confined to his chair. He had no doubt heard from Persinger that I played Lalo's *Symphonie*

espagnole, and he accompanied me, incredibly and accurately, in *pizzicato* notes on his Guarnerius. At the end of the movement, intriguingly he asked me to play a four octave arpeggio. This I did not play well, and his valuable comment was that I would do well to practice scales and arpeggios. I later took this to heart, but at that time I was too young to "waste" my time on exercises.

As for myself I wanted to study with a man to whom I had lost my heart and soul when I heard him two years earlier in San Francisco. Georges Enesco was the incarnation of music itself. Whatever music emanated from him it was something that communicated the whole gamut of our emotions in the authentic style of the period and the composer in a way so powerful none could resist. I had experienced this in San Francisco on his two visits when he had come to conduct his own symphony, as well as his great string octet arranged for orchestra, and to play the Brahms Concerto. The expressive beauty of his face and his romantic and powerful profile, stamped with a nobility I had never seen, transformed Enesco in my mind into the most inspired human being I have ever known. Although not a Gypsy, he understood their musical idiom better than almost anyone, composing a third sonata in the popular Romanian style—a miracle of notation. Any violinist who played this work rigorously according to his requirements would sound like a genuine Gypsy fiddler.

With my adoration in mind, and with my parents and sisters, I attended Enesco's next Paris concert, and my parents told me that if I wanted to study with him I should ask him myself. After the concert I stood in line and when my moment came I said simply

*E*verything about Ysaÿe was grandiose, huge, and magnified, and it is no accident that in this photograph he assumes the pose of Rodin's *Thinker*. Ysaÿe was so impressive that the violin seemed tiny in his hands. By his intensity, his power, and his elegance he was to the violin what Rostropovich is to the cello. I only met him once, at the end of his life, and he gave me brief, cautionary words of advice. However, I am in a sense his grandson, in learning terms, because he was the teacher of my first teacher, Louis Persinger.

"I would like to study with you." The epitome of courtesy, Enesco replied that he had to leave Paris at seven o'clock the next morning. I overcame my disappointment and in a final leap of boldness suggested that I come to see him very early. Accordingly I played for him at six a.m. and he gave me his blessing and his time ever since. He also refused to accept payment from my father. He had the most incredible musical memory I have ever known: I do not think he ever forgot anything he ever heard, played, or conducted.

His works are finally coming to prominence: alongside his better known *Romanian Rhapsodies*, his grandiose masterpiece, the opera *Oedipus* and his symphonies and quartets are now beginning to be played. That was his real musical vocation and he traveled with these scores, even composing at night after concerts. Yet he once said to me "I'm terribly lazy, because I dream of only one thing: lying stretched out in the summer in a Moldavian field listening to the buzz of insects."

The most phenomenal aspect, the most astonishing thing about this musical genius, was his prodigious memory. For instance he confessed that he knew by heart only fifty-eight volumes of the original edition of Bach. The ones that he did not remember were the fifty-ninth volume, quite simply because it was missing from his library, and the sixtieth, which was the index to the others. He could also play on the piano from memory the many operas of Wagner in a magnificent performance, singing, whistling, or grunting aloud the parts of the various characters. I think he adored Wagner because they were both made of the same romantic fiber, driven by the same brilliance of primordial creation.

*T*he essence of Enesco.
This photograph magnificently
illustrates his powers
of enchantment.
More than an interpreter,
Enesco was a visionary.
He went beyond the printed page
to see the very heart
of a work, its logic, its hidden
meaning, the creativity bursting
from within it.
He listened to the music before
he played it, and if he closes
his eyes here, it is to see all
the better the musical image
coming to him directly
from the composer. I had never
met a violinist like him.
He was the musician
of my dreams, and it was
with him that, at the age
of eight, I decided to work.

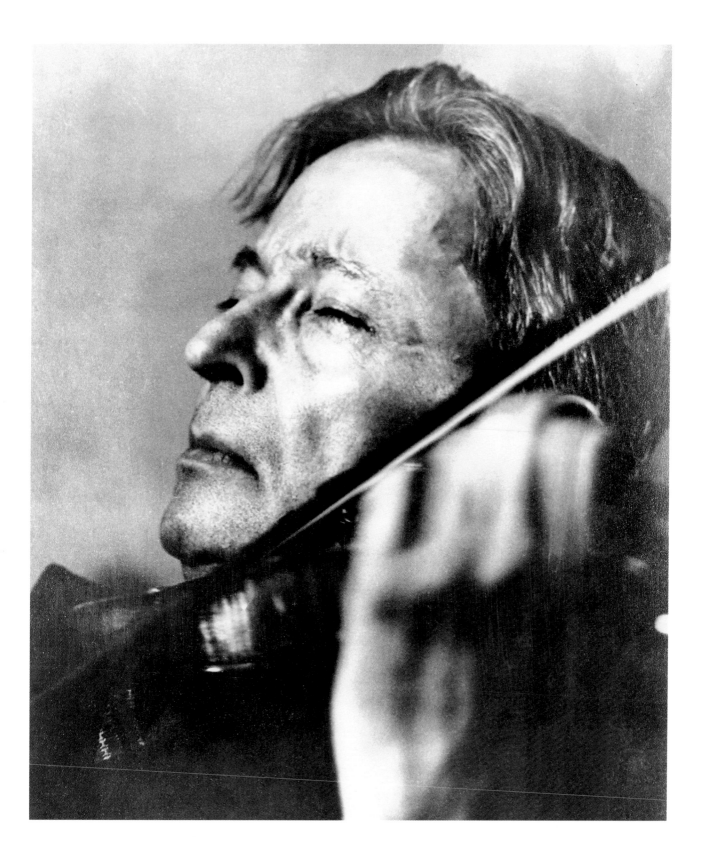

*E*nesco's genius

was such that all the musicians

of his day came to consult him.

He never made mistakes,

because he was able to see

and understand a work

in its entirety, whereas most

musicians simply look at fragments.

If today I have the capacity

to understand a score,

and to conduct an orchestra,

I owe it in large part to Enesco.

Enesco and the

Rosé Quartet, 1922.

One day Ravel arrived unexpectedly at Enesco's apartment in Paris, at 36 rue de Clichy, while I was having a lesson. It was customary for the publishers Durand et Fils to listen to a work before deciding whether to publish it (to us today this seems incredible that people who may or may not be able to judge could insist upon this). Ravel had just finished his *Sonata for Piano and Violin*, and he wanted Enesco to play it with him. Enesco courteously apologized for having to interrupt my lesson, and set about sight-reading this difficult work, stopping occasionally to ask for clarification. Then he suggested to Ravel that they repeat the piece: Ravel agreed. Enesco closed the score and played the piece from memory, without hesitation. Such an achievement is not just the result of musical

*E*nesco was not only capable

of playing the violin,

conducting an orchestra,

and composing music;

he was also a marvelous pianist.

My lessons with him

were extraordinary moments

of exchange, during which

he never spoke the language

of technique but only

the language of the heart,

of emotion, and of musical

intelligence.

In this photograph, his look

is not that of somebody reading

a score: by a process of instant

analysis he is here deciphering

the deep inner meaning

of the work.

Yehudi Menuhin

and George Enesco

at the Hôtel Majestic, Paris.

intelligence, nor of an intimate understanding of musical structure, but I am sure it is because Enesco knew music in his earliest years and could sing and imagine it long before he could read music or play the violin. He understood works from within, not as a stranger from the outside, but as one who already knew.

Enesco had nobility of spirit, and such generosity and loyalty, which could hardly be believed. In his early years he fell in love with one of the beauties of the Romanian court, Princess Cantacuzène, who was much older than he. But she was already married to a leading member of the Romanian aristocracy. Her husband, before he died, asked Enesco to promise he would look after her. She was already ailing when he finally married her, and he continued to look after her despite the enormous burden this represented for him. He did this without hesitation and with never a word of regret or rejection.

When I was reunited with him after the war in Bucharest (for he had stayed there during the war) he came to meet me at the airport, and as we were entering the city he made one of those puns at which he excelled, conveyed with a characteristic gesture, covering his mouth, which he made when he felt he let himself down: "C'est la Boue-qui-reste!" ("this is the mud that sticks!"). The same humor was displayed in the caricatures he drew.

Lessons with Enesco were moments of inspiration. He accompanied me on the piano and listened to my playing. Sometimes he would pick up his violin to show me something. He never made me work on the instrument from a technical point of view. He knew how to speak to my imagination, to my senses, and he understood that the language of discipline and dull

*I*t was in Enesco's homeland,
Romania, that I heard Gypsy
musicians for the first time.
Their music, their spontaneity,
their natural way of being
were an utter revelation to me.
The first violin (on the left)
has an expression of dreamy
abandon that is similar,
on another level,
to that of Enesco.
Almost transported, he listens
to the melody he is playing,
while his neighbor plays
the counter-rhythm.
The second man could
be defined as the archetype
of the second violin:
he has probably never played
a melody in his life, nor on
the beat; he is a specialist
in playing upbeats.
Behind them, a bass player
completes the trio,
while an impromptu dancer
with a cigarette in his mouth
lets his body speak,
under the amused eye
of an old grandfather.

work was not appropriate at that moment of my artistic development.

Enesco was inseparable from the Romanian soil from which he sprang and of which he was at once both fruit and expression. Through my contact with him, I in turn received the stamp and the indelible mark of that country and of its myriad musical idioms, for each valley had its own style in music, dress and traditions. Romania was a discovery for me: it was also an opportunity for strange encounters. For its nature, its way of life, and its legends had also fashioned my mother, who was born in the Crimea and had never been to Romania.

I am glad to have known the last remnant of a feudal age in which a tight structure and different functions were assumed by virtue of habit, heredity and without question. We all know of the injustices and inequalities that beset the inhabitants, but were those injustices any greater than those in our own societies today? They were not inequalities of money and power so much as of function and culture. No doubt the industrial age was incompatible with this social structure, yet there was an element of security and organic unity with nature which was still respected, except when some Russian landowner sold timber from the vast forests which he owned and the labor was provided by the souls "belonging" to the property. But in general I did not get the impression of exploitation in Romania, rather that the system supported a high level of cultivation in music and the arts. Enesco introduced my father and me to Gypsy violinists and this made a profound impression of spontaneity on me which guided me towards Stéphane Grappelli in jazz and towards Ravi Shankar in Indian classical music.

The cultural diversity of Europe at that time displayed an unbelievable wealth. There was as yet no drive towards commercial or technological expansion, and media and communications had not yet started to impose uniformity on all countries.

While the imposition of monocultures had proved disasterous for those unfortunate islands and domains under European control, transforming rich and balanced native habitats into factories for sugar, coffee, tea, tobacco, and all Western indulgences, Europe itself had no such affliction. It had after all accepted wave after wave of immigration and domination, and despite years of war and conflict on several occasions, had achieved a productive European unity, in the shape of the Holy Roman Empire and the Mediterranean world of the Renaissance. But although the European cultures cross-pollinated one other, each

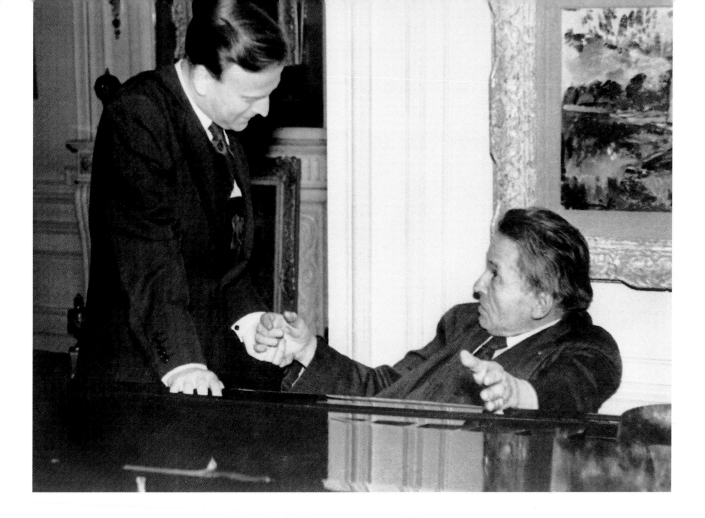

was still distinct, and nationalism had not yet attempted to impose a singular mold upon the different peoples.

It was not entirely in a spirit of joking that Antal Doráti, the great musician and composer, and a beloved friend, said in a reflective moment that Europe would do better to go back to these little areas, each with its own sentry boxes and borders, where people spent their time devising new uniforms and barriers, gates and frontiers, tolls and taxes. This would keep everyone happy and busy in endless gossip about neighboring fiefs and principalities, and life would probably be more secure and interesting than the vast new Europe we are currently attempting to construct. My aim is to restore that secure sense of independent cultural identity while collaborating with the community of cultures to greater purpose.

*W*henever he had free time from his tours, Enesco gave me lessons. His life was divided between his Paris apartment at 36 rue de Clichy and his Villa Luminisch in Romania. Since he was close to the Romanian royal family, Enesco had an unmistakeable elegance and a great social savoir–faire.

He had a romantic liaison with the Princess Cantacuzène, and eventually married her. His own room in the Villa was, however, monastic in its spareness, both in itself and by contrast with the wealth of velvet, tapestries, and cushions in the princess' apartments.

*A*lthough he had neither the poetry nor the passion of Enesco, Adolf Busch was nevertheless an essential link in the chain of my education. This representative of the pure and noble German tradition, who had somehow maintained the innocence of a young boy, provided me with a sense of rigor and discipline, as well as a deep understanding of German culture. He was a marvelous musician, he had his own quartet, and played a lot in chamber groups with his son-in-law, Rudolf Serkin. Busch was also a composer. One day, I found him sitting before a huge score with innumerable staves, which was printed specially for him.

*W*hen I left Sinaia, Enesco advised me to work with the great German violinist, Adolf Busch. He had decided that Busch's rigor would be a salutary counterweight to my effervescent temperament, and that a Germanic touch would have a stabilizing influence on me. Two years later, in 1929, my family and I went to live in Basel for two years. There I took lessons with Busch, and it is to him that I owe my deep respect for German culture. Without him, I would not have been able to understand and penetrate the spirit and heart of that music of mists and forests, of drama and contained passion. Once again, Enesco had known the right thing to do.

*B*ach, Handel, and Haydn
were all three musicians
who knew faith and good fortune.
They all attributed their inspiration
to God and had a certainty
of expression which was never
dogmatic. I cannot imagine either
Bach, Handel or Haydn having
self-doubts—indeed the greatest
composers could not bequeath
us their gift of life had
they not known the difference
between good and less good,
between perfection
and compromise. In looking
at their scores we recognize
the quality of uninterrupted
fluency, the absence of corrections,
even in the most complex works.
Their works convey a sense
of health and balance, a flow
of invention of the surprising
and unexpected, especially
in Haydn—the nearest
a human being can surely
approach to the divine.
Anonymous, *Portrait
of Joseph Haydn*, 1770.
Eisenstadt, Austria,
Haydn-Museum. Violin part
for Johann Sebastian Bach's
Missa Solemnis.
Leipzig, Bach-Archiv.

THE VIOLIN COMPOSER

*W*e have been composing and decomposing for billions of years, embodying constant transformations. This in itself is a creative process as it responds not only to the evolutionary principle of adaptation and survival of the fittest, but I am convinced also to the destiny of life— the yearning for knowledge and understanding which draws us towards that higher power we sometimes call God. Thus the pattern of transformation is dictated not only by physical survival but the spiritual and intellectual urge towards the light of awareness and consciousness, responsibility for growing choice and understanding. We constantly transform food

This picture too is an image
of serenity, happiness,
and certainty. It depicts a kind
of Garden of Eden where
everything is bursting with life:
fruit, flowers, fish, birds,
and human beings proliferate
in this cornucopia of nature
on the day of Creation.
Today we have lost this blessed
confidence in the world around
us. Composers as creators
no longer owe their inspiration
to the One above them,
but to their own personality,
character and environment.
There are few who can
transcend these specificities,
nor can they dispel anxiety.
Anonymous Flemish painter,
The Four Elements,
seventeenth century.
London, Gavin Graham Gallery.

into energy, observation into thought and action; and the urgency to create, to transform, drives the artist to the most unimaginable limits of expression and sublimation.

We can create but we cannot invent; nothing we make is totally new. If we design containers, locks and keys, or computers it is because the basic design exists in nature. Spiders have built nets and bridges; the albatross sails in the air like a glider; the human body transforms light, air, food and water into bone, muscle, tissue, memory and intellect; telepathy preceded electronic communication by telegraph. Yet in another way our creations are totally new in the sense that the recasting of the material, the new shape and experience are generated by processes which are not wholly natural. We are unable to create without drawing on the raw material which patterns the human mind. Music is perhaps the most extraordinary transformation of the intangible—thought and emotion—into the medium of sound. It is perhaps the greatest distance one can travel between the raw source and its expression in art. Musicians discovered that there were mathematical and rhythmical rules in the realm of sound, and these evolved into works as far removed from the original impulse as one can imagine.

How natural is music? We are born to it in the musical communication between the child and the parent. The child hears music first, and learns to judge by pitch, texture, and amplitude of vibrations. These are elements which fall short of speech but belong to the realm of music which describes subjective states of being.

However, music can also carry us to a different level, detached from actual raw experience but evoking its echo objectively. Such music is no longer mortal—it is informative, perhaps chastening, but enjoyable because it is removed from first experiences to a higher plane of reliving and recalling the echoes of those first impacts.

Music is therefore a transformation on to another level of organized sound of all that we feel deeply and compulsively, but which has in itself no shape or form. The composer transforms the secret vibrations of humankind, listening, deciphering and

*H*ere we have a fifteenth-century image which treats the art of the Muses, or *mousikê* in Greek. But this figure is merely an echo, a voice deriving from Orpheus or Apollo. From the Chinese and the Greek period we know that music was attributed to a god, or in China to a particular person, the minister to the Emperor Hung-ti who is said to have discovered the twelve notes of the octave established by a progression of perfect fifths. I wonder if he also discovered the Pythagorean comma? In Europe, monotheism usurped the varied origins of human creativity: there was no longer a god attributed to the sea, or to love, or to music. *Music*, from *A Treatise on the Liberal Arts*, fifteenth-century manuscript. Venice, Biblioteca Marciana.

Music seems, at its apogee, to link every other discipline. We have already noted that it is a therapy, and we know that it can be an expression of passion or mathematical precision. The great composer is the one who can give structure to passion, who can bring the repose of crystal clarity to the crucible of chaos, who can handle fire without being scorched. This is an ideal balance, and has its counterpoint in a society which tries to contain the uncontrollable by law, not always successfully. Bach was the synthesis of these opposites without which great achievements do not happen.

He could see the universe in a grain of dust, and he could also see the grain of dust in its uniqueness, as an indispensible part of the universe. For him nothing existed in isolation, but was part of a whole. His conception of the Preludes and Fugues as a whole, of his art of the fugue as a methodical progression dwarfs those who proceed from one uncertainty, or one fraction, to the next. Elias Gottlob Haussmann (1695–1774), *Portrait of Johann Sebastian Bach*, 1764. Leipzig, Museum der bildenden Künste.

transcribing this inner voice to make it audible to others. One might almost say that Beethoven became deaf in order better to hear the sounds he generated within his mind to the exclusion of all others. Anything that was foreign to that inner voice was of no importance. It is sad to think of all those Beethoven works the composer never actually heard—but his scores are testimony to his inner hearing. There are composers who do not hear what they write, but this was not the case with Beethoven, for he wrote what he heard. He had already suffered a certain sense of isolation; he had had to sacrifice so much he would have loved to enjoy and possess. Deafness was the ultimate barrier that emprisoned him in his own world. Music became his whole life and through the creative process of composing, the element within which he lived.

Beethoven's compositions are unique as they represent a sublime distillation of human experience, a universality, and a total resistance to personal description of any kind. Whereas in Mozart you can recognize the person, in Beethoven you recognize the universal

*M*usic can be summed up in these three figures: rhythm, wind, and strings. Each of the musicians here has his gaze turned to the sky, as if seeing a bird or a divinity. There is no introspection. The sole aim of the music is to entertain, to produce joy and happiness. Carried along by their exhilarating improvisation, these instrumentalists are playing purely for pleasure, with neither score nor prior rehearsal.

Three Musicians:
Vina, Flute, and Tambour,
from *The History of the Mongols,*
seventeenth-century manuscript.
Venice, Biblioteca Marciana.

principle: indeed he reduces even the most basic ornamentation to the essential. He works not by adding to a phrase, nor by embellishment, rather he takes away the unnecessary, that which is not absolutely essential. There are examples of this in the second movement of his *Violin Concerto*: in the third bar he omits all the passing notes which already occurred in the first movement, in the minor version of the opening subject.

In his preludes, the *Well-Tempered Klavier*, and the fugues, Bach reveled in ornamentation, improvisation and romantic abandon. Pablo Casals was convinced that Bach must have had Gypsy blood because of the improvisation in the chromatic fantasy. He felt the same about the *adagio* from the *Sonata in G Minor for Solo Violin*. Indeed Bach's family may have originally come from Hungary, and there was a wild, quite untameable element to his passionate improvisations, which he used as introductions to the mighty fugues and the other movements of the sonatas and suites.

All great composers must control the huge sweep of their concept. Bach composed the six sonatas and partitas for solo violin in a sequence laid out in advance which takes the natural notes thus: G, B, A, D, C, E, leaping by thirds. He had to go from A to D because otherwise he would have to repeat the B. One can appreciate the sense of wholeness of the sonatas by looking at Bach's manuscripts. Where he was left with space for a single stave or two, which he drew with a five-pointed pen, he never failed to begin the next sonata at the bottom of the page. This was not because of a desire to save paper—it was because in the fluency of the concept Bach knew the key of the next sonata and preferred to think of music horizontally rather than vertically, a relic of the great contrapuntal age that preceded him. Bach's *Art of the Fugue* surpasses anything the most sophisticated computer could invent today. The theme for this colossal piece was given by Frederick the Great of Prussia, himself a composer who was extremely well versed in music—I doubt there are many heads of state today who could give a fugal theme to a composer. In the harshness and hostility of Bach's world—and of our own—the creation of music provides a means of resistance, an affirmation of life, and a preservation from the madnesses and barbarities which threaten our minds and our lives.

Like Beethoven, Bach also spoke of universalities but in terms of a suffering savior who suffered for all and who deprived the individual of the right to claim any suffering for himself. This is a submissive, resigned approach which we find difficult to understand, but which no doubt held society together at that time. It is a faith that insists upon patience and acceptance; it is unsentimental and yet compassionate.

*I*nstead of the taut instrument ready to vibrate, here the violin is soft and melting, like a piece of material. This process of liquefaction and decay in objects is one of Dalí's favorite themes. We also sense a degree of disgust emanating from the woman framed in the broken wall. Is it an image of the madness that could overtake our society if music no longer offered a solid bastion against violence? Is it the spirit of destruction that sometimes haunts the wives of violinists? The Catalan painter's delirious imagination opens the door to all kinds of interpretations. Salvador Dalí (1904–1989), *Masochistic Instrument*, 1933–34. Switzerland, private collection.

*T*he Italian school originated
with Arcangelo Corelli.
He knew how to discipline
the art of the violin
in an era when virtuoso playing
may have tended to a libertine
and untamed form.
And the sophisticated art
of using freedom was not known
to all violinists.
Anonymous, *Portrait of Corelli.*
Naples, Conservatorio di Musica
di San Pietro.

GREAT COMPOSERS

*T*hroughout my life I have known many contemporary composers. In my early years, however, I was interpreting the violin's heritage—written by composers I could not speak to or consult. Yet it is remarkable to what extent one can become acquainted with a composer from his music alone.

Invariably the violin is felt to belong to the melodic *bel canto* of Italian composers. What on the score looks almost too simple turns out inevitably to be masterful and totally satisfying. Arcangelo Corelli (1653–1713), the most eminent composer of the Italian school, was a renowned violinist. His sonatas support the edifice that the Italian Baroque erected to the glory of the violin, and he opened the way for numerous other violinists to compose for the violin: Tomaso Albinoni (1671–1750) and, above all, Antonio Vivaldi (1678–1741)—to whom we owe the form of the violin concerto. Francesco Geminiani (1687–1762), Pietro Antonio Locatelli (1695–1764), Giuseppe Tartini (1692–1770), and many others shone with virtuoso talents. They both played and conducted the works they composed, thus simultaneously developing the literature for the violin and the instrument's technique.

In those days the art of providing ornamentation as you played, of improvising the melodic *fioriture* on the bare melody, was something every musician knew. In the same spirit the harpsichord player improvised the counterpoint in accordance with the harmony as it was indicated on the figured bass. This creative element diminished as composers indicated in ever greater detail the notes they wished the performer to play. And the repetition of sections with different

*A*ntonio Vivaldi was known as the "red priest", director of a large orphanage for girls of "good family" in Venice, the Pietà. They were "good" children too and from him they received a wonderful musical training.

They played the double bass and conducted and played the solo concerti, no doubt in perfect style and with great beauty.

As director of the school Vivaldi composed for all instruments— some 530 compositions according to the requirements and the musicians available.

He was highly regarded by Bach himself, who transcribed several of the Venetian composer's concertos for organ and harpsichord. It was, incidentally, in rediscovering Bach in the nineteenth century that people revived the forgotten works of Vivaldi.

Anonymous, *Portrait of Vivaldi*. Bologna, Museo Bibliografico Musicale.

Mozart's operas have inspired
all kinds of stagings.
They are highly symbolic,
mostly of human valor
and greatness of spirit,
and in the hands of contemporary
directors who want to leave
their stamp on the work,
this opens the door to the most
outlandish settings. Here,
in the course of the quintet
in *The Magic Flute*,
the three Ladies of the Night are
preparing to give Prince Tamino
(in blue) the magic flute which
will enable him to repel the forces
of evil. As for Papageno (right),
the bird man, he is given
the glockenspiel which has
equal powers. Mozart's music is
a miracle of the transfiguration
of life by music and symbolism,
and it is universal in the sense
that audiences around the world
find it applies to their condition
and their civilization,
however distant it may be from
the elegant European salons
of the eighteenth century.
Wolfgang Amadeus Mozart's
The Magic Flute, directed
by Bob Wilson, 14 February 1994.
Paris, Opéra Bastille.

ornamentation in each section, which was the practice in the Baroque, gave way to the continous, wider architecture of a more massive composition. The cadenza too, at the end of the movement when the soloist was expected to play alone to sum up the themes of the piece, was replaced by a written cadenza composed in detail by the composer himself, thus denying the last vestige of improvisation to the performer. To restore the quality of improvisation which should inform every performance, even of works we all know, I believe that the Italian works for the violin should form the basic repertoire of the beginner.

In a later generation, Johann Sebastian Bach (1685–1750), Joseph Haydn (1732–1809), and Wolfgang Amadeus Mozart (1756–1791) were also accomplished violinists. While composing, they already had in mind an idea of the fingering or bowing that would be required to perform the work.

Mozart's compositions, some of the most incredible examples of the transformation of life by art, offer us not only a velvety smoothness of sound, but also an underlying intensity of passion. I shall always remember the image by which Enesco described Mozart's universe during one of our lessons in Paris. He compared Mozart's music to the smiling and sunny slopes of a vineyard planted on the sides of an active volcano. He also said that every note should be played as a syllable, and that it had to carry within it the inflections of a human voice. When I went with my father to hear Mozart operas at the Salzburg Festival, I understood this—that each note was a presence, each phrase was a gesture, and each scene was a human moment with universal relevance. The same had to be true for Mozart's instrumental music. It

*I*t is rare to see Paganini playing like this, in the confined atmosphere of a bourgeois salon. We know that he preferred the vastness of concert halls, where delirious crowds could gather round to applaud him. Well before the celebrity era, Paganini invented the one-man show. He was the first violinist in history to lead an independent career as a virtuoso, enjoying an adulation that was close to the supernatural and earning a considerable amount of money in the process. But he was also generous and helped Berlioz whom he admired. No less an artist than Liszt recognized the genius of Paganini. Niccolo Paganini was also a very gifted composer: witness his 24 *Caprices* which are as demanding of the violinist as they are inventive musically. Rumor and gossip said that he had made a pact with the devil, and he very wisely did nothing to discourage such useful publicity. Annibale Gatti (1827–1909), *A Concert by Paganini*. Florence, Galleria d'Arte Moderna.

seemed obvious to me that when I played a Mozart composition I would have to respect and express this basic vocal quality. Like a shore from which the tide has ebbed, I have long preserved the traces of these images and these sensations.

In the nineteenth century, Niccolo Paganini (1782–1840), and even the great Felix Mendelssohn (1809–1847) belonged to this tradition of composer–violinists, or on occasion violinist–composers, and wrote works that were designed to highlight their technical virtuosity. Closer to our own time in the same tradition we find Henri Vieuxtemps (1820–1881), Henryk Wieniawski (1835–1880),

CLAUDIUS

This engraving portrays only one aspect of the Beethoven legend. He knew the vicissitudes of life and the tragedies. This image somehow looks posed and contrived—a product of the imagination. He has left his mark on humanity who recognize him as a human being of great passion, equally capable of sacred fury and of an almost transcendent serenity. He did not leave the world a better place than he knew it, but certainly a richer one. Ludwig van Beethoven, engraving after a painting by Hermann Junker.

Édouard Lalo (1823–1892), Pablo de Sarasate (1844–1908), and Antonín Dvořák (1841–1904).

Peter Ilich Tchaikovsky (1840–1893), Sergei Prokofiev (1891–1953), and Béla Bartók (1881–1945), although not themselves violinists, were very close to the violin, because the instrument was deeply rooted in their cultural traditions. Their works are thus perfectly written for it.

Among the exceptions to the rule, we have two notable figures. Neither Beethoven nor Brahms was a violinist. In order to write his opus 77, *Concerto for Violin and Orchestra in D major*, Johannes Brahms (1833–1897) consulted his great friend, the violinist Joachim, at length. In the manuscript, it is not difficult to spot the influence, advice, and contributions of Joachim, particularly in the cadenzas. This did not prevent Brahms' detractors from saying, at the work's first performance, that this was not a concerto for the violin, but a concerto *against* the violin.

Ludwig van Beethoven (1770–1827), like Brahms, was a pianist. At the time he was writing his opus 61, *Concerto for Violin and Orchestra in D major*, he had asked the advice of a German violinist, Franz Klement, who went on to perform the work in Vienna in 1806. But the weight of the "pianistic" model is perhaps more noticeable in Beethoven than in Brahms. Thus in this concerto the phrasings are in a sense notional, and the performer may modify them, as long as the spirit of the composer is respected. By this I mean that some of the phrases indicated in the score are so long that no bow in the world would be able to play so slowly. In the marvelous melody of the second movement, for example, there is a phrase extending across two bars that would be almost impossible to play. The violinist can respect the idea of the phrase, but must nevertheless interrupt the composer's phrasing. Yet these difficulties and the solutions they necessitate sometimes make it possible to transmit the composer's ideal better; they inspire strokes of inspiration that accentuate the brilliance of the composer's genius, just as a good setting can intensify the sparkle of a precious stone. Herein lies the magic of interpretation.

Composers today have such a wealth of possibilities at their disposal, such a multitude of means and languages, that it becomes difficult to escape from a referential system and to build a personal language. Once there was such a thing as a European music—Baroque music. Of course there were Italian, French, German, and English variants, but generally speaking the music belonged to the same system, each composer impressing on this familiar background the particular mark of personal imagination. All Baroque music was played with the same instruments: Bach wrote keyboard arrangements for Vivaldi concertos, and the Venetian style was imitated throughout Germany.

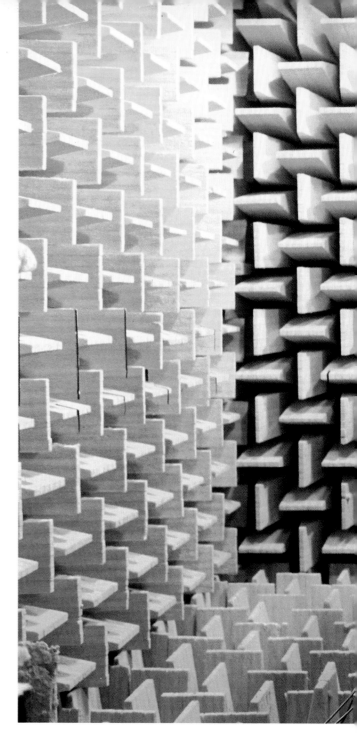

The he absurdity
of the soundproofed room.
This sophisticated equipment,
which enables one to make
recordings in a hermetic box
without the interference
of so-called "parasitic" noise,
runs contrary to the very spirit
of music and betrays
our obsession with one criterion
at the expense of all others.
It is terrible to think
of music being isolated like this,
cut off from all context,
background, and sources.

Cultural exchange was part of the order of things, because music was a universal language that spoke to audiences of different nationalities; it had abolished frontiers.

Modern composers, by contrast, face almost unlimited choices. Their music can be acoustic one day, electronic the next, and *musique concrète* the day after. It may also develop as collages of different kinds of sound. The range of folk music on which composers are now able to draw is immense. Thanks to recordings, they are familiar with the music of India, Cuba, Africa, or South America. It is as if music today were trying to explore the gaps between the rigid categories of the past, like a painter who goes beyond the basic colors to experiment with the full range of shades. In this never-ending search, in this continual state of agitation, it is very hard to find stability and calm. This is why modern music so often lacks serenity, elegance, and devotion—in short everything that is also missing from our world—although there is a religious fervor, solidly rooted in the spirit of its inhabitants, that still inspires the creation of masses and oratorios in Poland, and also provides isolated examples of those feelings we cannot find in our cities.

Encounters

*I*t is not only a privilege but it also gives me the greatest satisfaction to work with a living composer. I am extremely fortunate in that I have been able to work with some of the greatest including Georges Enesco and Béla Bartók.

My very first encounter with a "live" composer was with Ernest Bloch (1880–1959) who was at that time living in San Francisco, as the head of the conservatory. We had met at the appartment of Mr. Lichtenstein, the first viola of the San Francisco Symphony, and I played at this gathering, aged seven. A few days later Bloch knocked at my door, looking for all the world like an Old Testament prophet, and handed me, the ink still wet on the paper, his *Avodah*, ("sacred labor" in Hebrew), a short piece with piano accompaniment. Imagine my joy to receive such a tribute from a living composer.

Bloch loved going back to his native Switzerland and photographing himself against the great mountains and glaciers, lending himself a presence and authority which derived from the magnificence of nature itself. Like Bartók he took a particular interest in folklore and folk music and although he had no Native American connections he spent some time in New Mexico in order to become acquainted with the indigenous Native American music and dance. Inspired by this experience he introduced the musical influences he had found into the slow movement of his *Violin Concerto* which I later recorded.

When we met in Paris, Bloch proudly showed me an exercise book in which he had written counterpoint and fugues for eight voices. He felt his counterpoint needed improvement and did not compose for a year while doing this in anticipation of composing his sacred Jewish service.

It was impressive to see a great composer deciding to do exercises for a whole year. We remained friends until his death: his two works for solo violin, his last works, are dedicated to me.

The composer I felt closest to was Georges Enesco, with whom I worked during my first period in Paris from 1927 to 1928, during my studies with him from 1931 to 1936, and later once again. On his concert tours Enesco would travel with the score of *Oedipus* and would spend nights bent over the unfinished score, working on it (Edmond Fleg, the poet and

---

*E*rnest Bloch had the appeal of a prophet. He expressed himself as a prophet, too, to such an extent that nobody dared interrupt when he was speaking. He maintained a direct dialogue with God, praying and at the same time calling Him to account in the Jewish tradition. A form of reciprocity and bargain—if I worship you, you must give me something in return. It is not the plea to a merciful god, but rather it is the demand for attention and direct intercession from an all-powerful and chastising god who often had to be instructed in the bestowal of mercy. It is always a difficult problem to apportion mercy with punishment. I loved Ernest Bloch and his music, and recently conducted his *Jewish Mass* in St Paul's Cathedral in London—a great example of ecumenism. Ernest Bloch and Yehudi Menuhin.

---

scholar who wrote the libretto for *Oedipus* did the same for Bloch's opera, *Macbeth*). I first heard *Oedipus* in Paris in 1938, at its première at the Paris Opera House, and later in Bucharest. It is hauntingly beautiful, a poetic piece with a last act or epilogue as a form of resurrection. With my sister I often played his third sonata which is written in a popular Romanian style. Outstanding in its triumphal way it combines the playing of a Gypsy with the strict form of a sonata. The notation is extraordinary: anyone who obeys implicitly the instructions will sound like a Gypsy violinist.

There was never any doubt in my mind about Enesco's greatness, his musical knowledge, his command of repertoire, his wonderful qualities as a teacher and a human being. His compositions are once again coming into fashion, as Lawrence Foster and

Sir Simon Rattle become his greatest exponents: Foster has recorded most of Enesco's works and Simon Rattle is utterly captivated.

Antal Doráti, a conductor and a friend, had introduced me to Bartók's works, and so it was in 1943 that I included two pieces by this great composer in the program of my winter tour. They were two glorious pieces—greater than any other contemporary works:

the *First Sonata for Piano and Violin* and the *Second Violin Concerto*. We played the Concerto with Dmitri Mitropoulos in Minneapolis, but before playing the sonata with Adolph Baller at Carnegie Hall, I wanted to seek Bartók's advice and criticisms. A meeting was arranged at the house of a mutual friend, who was an old friend of Toscanini, and also a violinist. I arrived early to find Bartók already seated in an armchair next

*B*artók's last years were marked by leukaemia, his skin was like stretched parchment, he was very pale but an indomitable spirit maintained his uncompromising presence and values. Only his eyes betrayed his burning soul and his critical assessment of life and the living. Béla Bartók in his house in Budapest.

iceberg—the most encouraging words I have ever heard. When we had finished the second and third movements Bartók then wanted to see what I understood of the concerto I had performed in Minneapolis. There had been no orchestra, so naturally I only played certain passages. He asked my opinion of one particular phrase in the first movement, which is repeated many times.

I said: "It's chromatic, and it's different each time, each time with a different succession of notes."

"Exactly," he said. "I used the twelve notes of the octave. I wanted to show Schönberg that one can use the twelve notes in sequence and still remain tonal." Indeed the tone rows had the most fascinating shapes, balanced and expressive and each one is wholly different—one alone might serve Schönberg or Alban Berg for a whole opera!

It was on that occasion that I asked Bartók to compose a solo violin work for me. Wanting to be modest and equally not to tax him, I asked only for a small composition. A year later however I received an extraordinary work, the opus 117, *Sonata for Solo Violin*, the greatest since Bach. Fortunately I had the opportunity of playing it almost immediately at Carnegie Hall in November 1944 with the composer present. The Carnegie Hall public was unstinting in its applause, enthusiasm, and admiration for the composer.

Bartók was very close to nature and understood much about the primitive roots of civilizations. With his friend and compatriot Zoltán Kodály he traveled through the Balkans, Turkey and North Africa, recording ancient tribal music on to primitive cylinders and then cataloguing them in perfect order at Columbia University, who engaged Bartók for the job some years

to the piano, the music on his lap and a pencil in hand, waiting. At that time he uttered not a single unnecessary word: he was already suffering from leukaemia and was saving his strength. There was nothing to do but unpack the violin and play. When we finished, Bartók rose to his feet and said "I did not think that music could be played like that until long after the composer was dead." It was like the melting of an later. At the end of his life, Bartók's last professional offer came from the University of Washington in Seattle, an invitation to study the music of the Native American in the Northwest. But Bartók was ill and in the summer of 1943 he was not even able to visit us at our home, Los Gatos, in California. He died in 1945.

Bartók's commitment to children mirrored that of other composers—Britten, Kodály, Leopold Mozart. All children who learn the piano should begin with his *Mikrokosmos*. Designed for beginners, these are six volumes of perfectly graded, very easy pieces, infallibly beautiful and free of period taste, wonderful for the ear and offering a superb perspective on harmony. It is a perfect introduction to music. His forty-four *Duets for Two Violins*, opus 98, also evoke the folk material of his own compositions. His greatest contributions to music are his string quartets which become ever more abstract and disembodied in the style of Beethoven, yet never losing the Hungarian and above all else the composer's stamp.

*I*t was Fred Geisberg, then one of the directors of HMV, who in 1932 sent me Sir Edward Elgar's (1857–1934) *Violin Concerto* together with a photograph of this most beloved of English composers. This was too great a thrill, and even though I had never played it I immediately loved the concerto and replied that I would record it. Six weeks later our neighbor, Paul Vian, my father and I drove from our home in Ville d'Avray to Calais. We were met on the other side of the English Channel by the grand old Rolls Royce belonging to Harold Holt, my manager in London. On this lovely summer's day we were driven to Grosvenor House where a piano had been installed in our room.

*B*artók was as methodical an academic as he was impassioned and genial a composer. In the top photograph, standing before the miraculous apparatus that was the phonograph, he is recording one by one the villagers of Danázs in Hungary. This was in 1907. The session is well organized: on the right, are the people who are going to sing, and, on the left, those who have already sung. At the invitation of Columbia University in New York years later, Bartók compiled a detailed classification of these folk songs, which are based on the intervals and rhythm of the first bar. With this same concern for getting back to origins, we see him (in the bottom photograph) working a hurdy-gurdy. This folk instrument is the exact opposite of the violin, because it is played with a round bow that rubs continually against the strings. Bartók was presumably interested in hearing how the instrument sounded and in understanding how it was used.

The pianist Ivor Newton arrived first, and Elgar himself shortly afterwards. Elgar was a most gentlemanly, grandfatherly person, who did not, to my teenaged eye, look in the least like a composer. Until then I had only known the obvious Old Testament types— poetical, prophetical and hardly mistakeable for anything else. But I learned then that you cannot fathom the depths of an Englishman, who may turn out to be often very sensitive or romantic, despite first appearances.

So we began playing and we had scarcely reached the second subject when Elgar said: "You play marvelously. That will be perfect, but it's such a lovely day... I'm going to the races!" He left, and I had no idea

if my interpretation would please him or not. The recording began the following Monday, and to my relief it went like a dream, and both of us were very happy. I had never played with such a large orchestra and had never seen a composer/conductor bring so much out of the orchestra with so little gesture or apparent effort. The concerto had been written in the early part of the century and originally dedicated to Fritz Kreisler, but on the score Elgar gave me he had written in his own pen "and also to Yehudi Menuhin." That was a treasured tribute I shall always remember.

I had played the piece for Enesco a week previously and—in a fine example of Enesco's understanding of the nature of a work—he had stressed to me its profound Englishness; and that for the second theme I needed to add a mixture of "distilled" Romanticism and moderation, simplicity and affection. In any case I grasped the full significance of that criticism over the years. Later the same year I played the work in public at the Royal Albert Hall with Elgar conducting, preceded by the Mozart and Beethoven concertos conducted by Sir Thomas Beecham. It was a grand occasion and the first time I had played an English work in public: the setting of the Royal Albert Hall was wonderful and there was as usual a packed house. It was perhaps the one occasion which wedded me most firmly to the English people and established me as part of the family of this island race, who have made me ever more welcome over the years.

I was determined to introduce the concerto to Paris, however, and decided to put it on my next program at the Salle Pleyel the following spring. Elgar came to stay at Ville d'Avray with my family, and he became a firm favorite of my sisters and indeed of all

In appearance, Sir Edward Elgar was a cross between a country squire and a grandfather. This photograph dates from 1932, when I was in London to record, under the composer's direction, his magnificent *Violin Concerto* (I am holding the score). Everything went calmly, serenely, and harmoniously. It was a fine example of the *sang froid* and sobriety which still characterizes the English team spirit—at least most of the time!

of us. I remember my mother making onion soup for Elgar's breakfast as a cure for his ulcers—I was astonished to think that a man so self-possessed, quiet, and sporting had ulcers!

The concert went superbly—Enesco rehearsed generously and Elgar took over at the dress rehearsal. My only regret of Elgar's four-day visit is that I did not accompany Elgar when he visited Delius at Grez-sur-Loing near Fontainebleau. By then Delius was paralyzed and almost wholly dependent on his alter ego, Eric Fenby, who wrote down his compositions for him. Later, with Eric Fenby, I recorded Delius's *Three Sonatas for Vioin and Piano,* and with Paul Tortelier the *Concerto for Violin and Cello* and the *Concerto for Violin.*

In England I enjoyed wonderful opportunities to get to know many English composers, my closest relationship being with Benjamin Britten (1913–1976). Ben invited me to play at his festivals in Aldeburgh every year, but our first meeting had been before he had returned to his beloved Suffolk. I had just returned from the United States and we met at a party given by his publishers, Boosey and Hawkes. This was 1945 and I was soon off to Germany to play at the former concentration camps and displaced persons'

camps, including Belsen. I had already arranged for Gerald Moore to accompany me, but Ben pleaded to go too on what was to be a tour of the British Zone of Germany. Britten had not shared the experience of the war in his home country and he needed to be part of an atmosphere which had been both shattering and inspiring. Gerald Moore understood and gracefully remained behind. Ben and I went to the camps without

rehearsing, and he proved to be a great accompanist, not only for the sonatas, but also the concerti and salon pieces which complete a violin program.

We played for the former slave labor of the camps—for the Jews and Gypsies who had survived the Nazi genocide, and who had been found in appalling conditions by the British troops. We arrived after Belsen had been razed to the ground, and the

Sir Thomas Beecham was the epitome of the genial English amateur, more professional even than the professional. He had a way of mocking the pomposity and pontification of the "great musician." When conducting in Australia he promised a dozen rehearsals but at the end of the first he said "Well, gentlemen, we'll meet at the concert." When asked what of the other rehearsals, he said he feared it could only get worse. He was the archetypal gentleman, and witticisms and anecdotes about him abound. But beyond this, Beecham was an inspired musician who excelled in Mozart, discovered Sibelius and could draw the maximum from an orchestra. From left to right: Sir Edward Elgar, Yehudi Menuhin, and Sir Thomas Beecham, 1932.

The extraordinary thing about the English school of composition is its essential Englishness—the English never went in for continental fashions. One might say that Elgar was the most German of English composers, yet he remained true to his native countryside and people. In the same way Sir Michael Tippett (b. 1905), Sir Peter Maxwell Davies (b. 1934), Sir Lennox Berkeley (1903–1989), and Ralph Vaughan Williams (1872–1958) are recognisably English, that is contrapuntal, melodious, and shy of any exaggeration, however intense their feeling might be.

*I*n 1945 while the war was still raging in the Far East I was invited by colleagues to go to Moscow where I met Dmitri Shostakovitch (1906–1975), and Aram Khachaturian (1903–1978), the latter through David Oistrakh. Shostakovitch was an intensely shy person, oppressed by the horrific regime which had already banned some of his works. His genius was such that he remained the voice of the people and was even tolerated by the regime after a fashion. I found it hard to imagine that such a timid person could be the composer of such shatteringly powerful music. We established a close relationship which continued when we met subsequently in Prague, London, and New York.

The very first person I met in Budapest after the war in 1946 was Zoltán Kodály (1882–1967). We became great friends and I asked him if he would compose a piece for me. I offered him a fee, payable per page. However, he refused my cheque saying that he was thriving well enough on the public's "bad taste," but that he would compose a piece for me during a cruise he was to take with his wife Emma, who

survivors have been transferred to the military camp which had an excellent hospital and every comfort—including crystal chandeliers beneath which the Nazi officers had danced while horror and disease spread in the adjoining camp. I hope that the music we played brought these people some image of the civilization which had abandoned them. I have since heard from hundreds of the survivors from all parts of the world.

Benjamin Britten and the tenor Peter Pears, composer and interpreter, complemented each other in every way. The literary and somewhat ecclesiastical Peter inspired and interpreted Ben's musical creations. Peter was always calm and serene, while Ben lived in a state of constant anxiety and tension. Ben's house was close to his beloved sea in Suffolk and he could compose best in that setting. Many great British composers like Vaughan Williams and Peter Maxwell Davies of another younger generation, needed that touch of sea with land to ignite their imaginations.

Kenneth Green, *Portrait of Benjamin Britten and Peter Pears*, 1943. London, National Portrait Gallery.

was then well over one hundred years old. Ultimately, Emma appointed her successor, Shary, who has become in her turn a devoted widow, perpetuating the memory of her husband.

I always associate Igor Stravinsky (1882–1971) with Picasso: both had incredible versatility, and could move from one style to another, remaining master of each. I recorded his *Concerto in D Major* for television with the New York Orchestra. The precision and clarity of his work were a product of his craftsmanship and unfailing ear, which like the eye of a jeweler could shape the facets of a diamond to maximum brilliance, whether he was composing in neo-classical dodeca-phonic, or deriving inspiration from Russian folk music. Stravinsky was also humorous and had an incisive personality: he was in particular very clever in exploiting his royalties by regularly reissuing a new edition of his works with just a few notes changed! His mastery of music and of life gave his natural wit a certain

Shostakovich was tortured not only by nature but even more so by the regime which presumed to dictate the style in which he should compose. Such was his integrity and genius, however, that he achieved greatness in the tragedy of his music, in the bitterness and scorn of his *scherzi* and the overall power of his truly continental music. By this I mean the same spaciousness as Tchaikovsky and the other Russians knew in their very nature.

He became a very close friend and an inspiration to Ben Britten and Rostropovich.
Iosif A. Serebrjanyj,
Portrait of Dmitri Shostakovich, 1964. Moscow, Tretyakov Gallery.

cutting edge. One story tells of when he received a telegram from a group in New York who had commissioned a work. The telegram said that they were thrilled, were sure it would have a great success but that it would have an even more resounding success if he agreed to cuts in a certain place. Stravinsky replied that he would be quite satisfied with a "great" success!

All these qualities won him the admiration and affection of Nadia Boulanger, the great twentieth-century teacher of composition, who has formed creators as diverse as Aaron Copland (1900–1990), Sir Lennox Berkeley, and Jean Françaix (b. 1912). She worshipped Stravinsky and her greatest test came when he adopted the dodecaphonic method. After much soul-searching—Boulanger never really approved of this rather arbitrary system—she finally felt able to continue her worship into this new domain.

*K*hachaturian

was beloved not only by his

fellow Armenians but by

the whole of the Russian people.

All his work vibrates

with the color, the exuberance,

even the recklessness of his native

people and land.

Like the music of other great

composers, it draws on its folk

traditions, and that oriental

lyricism which derives

from Mohammedan traditions.

His *Violin Concerto*

has become one of the war-horses

of the younger generation.

In the early 1950s I was invited to play the Sibelius Concerto for the composer's ninetieth birthday in Helsinki, and I took the opportunity to visit Jean Sibelius (1865–1957) in his typical Finnish wooden house in the forest. It was a lovely day and we were having a pleasant conversation on his balcony, when for no conceivable reason—unless he wanted me to know the answer—Sibelius asked me: "Who is the greatest composer of the twentieth century?" Of course I could not say anything: to say "Sibelius" would have been too rude, and to invoke anyone else would have been too insulting. Fortunately, to my immense relief he answered for me—"Bartók"—and I could have hugged him! He told me that he had known Bartók as a fellow student in Berlin and had loved him too. I was very happy when he expressed his approval and satisfaction with the concert; he had not been able to come, but had listened to the broadcast on the radio.

I also worked with Darius Milhaud (1892–1974), a French composer resident in California. He was capable of great feats of concentration: once in the midst of an animated conversation at my home he composed a four-movement duet for two violins, which I played immediately with my colleagues assembled there. I have also been fortunate to work with the Israeli composers, Ödön Partos, Ben Haim, and Dov Selzer; Arnold Cooke from England, Ross Lee Finney and Roy Harris both from the USA. From Finney I commissioned a *Sonata for Solo Violin* for the opening of the American pavilion at the Brussels World's Fair nearly forty years ago. He too used the dodecaphonic system, and readily agreed that one could cover the music paper quicker with that system… I skipped one bar by mistake but to my relief Finney did not notice.

At the Bath Festival with my sister Hephzibah and Maurice Gendron I premiered a trio by Alexander Goehr. But perhaps the most difficult piece composed at my request was by a pupil of Peter Maxwell Davies, a sonata with piano. It had the most exacting sequences of rhythmic complications. I could see that the young composer was not at all pleased by my efforts, although he did manage to keep his good humor. I asked if his father was a mathematician by any chance and he replied, "Yes, indeed!"

Despite every change of style, and despite a recent period of composition which has been generally unmelodic, the violin, like the human voice, still demands a form of music which is singable and therefore moving and inspiring. In these days given to confrontation and violence, we are fortunate to have the violin as our companion.

*T*his painting shows a man whose work is done. What we see here is not a composer still quivering with the vibrancy of creation, but a man who recognized his creative term and enjoys the tranquillity in the second part of life which is ruminative and happy. Yet in the creative incarnation of his life, he voiced the torment of his people.

It was at this period of his life that I had the good fortune to meet Sibelius, an encounter which won my total admiration, since in answer to his own question, who is the greatest composer of the century, he replied, "Bartók." Teodor Schalin, *Portrait of Jean Sibelius*, 1952. Turku, Finland, Sibeliusmuseum.

At the summit of the sacred
Mount Parnassus we find Apollo,
god of the arts and more
particularly the god of music—
the invention of the lute
is attributed to him.
At his feet is a bow,
the ancestor of the violin, because
Apollo is also the archer-god.
To his right is Pegasus,
the winged horse and symbol
of poetic inspiration.
To his left, the Castalian Springs
pour forth into a flowery stream
that flows down to bathe
the feet of the Muses.
Beneath the benevolent eye
of their protector,
these goddesses have gathered
to make music.
School of Fontainebleau,
sixteenth century,
from an engraving
by Giorgio Ghisi, *Parnassus*.
Aix-en-Provence, Musée Granet.
In Western music,
which is based on harmony,
the various instrumental lines all
need each other to create
the basic quartet of voices.
G. Bella, *The Violinists* (detail).
Venice, Palazzo
Querini-Stampalia.

PARTNERS

*I*n the musical world preceding the harmonic era
the violin was a lone voice, and as in Indian
music it sang to the rhythm of feet and drum.
But in our increasingly multi-voiced, collaborative
world of parliaments and symphony orchestras the
heights of musical expression are to be found where
four-stringed instruments join forces to form quartets
or other close musical partnerships.

In this new world the keyboard instrument as
well as the orchestra becomes a partner or foil to the
soloist. Inevitably the violinist is accompanied by the
pianist to produce harmonic dimensions which the
violinist alone cannot achieve. A few works for solo

*P*artners but also members
of the same family....
I have had the good fortune
to be surrounded by two sisters
who are very dear to me
(Hephzibah on the left,
and Yaltah on the right),
and my son Jeremy.
This musical and family reunion
took place around the Mozart
Triple Concerto, which I am here
preparing to conduct.
Hephzibah and Jeremy
have been very special partners
in my career as a violinist.
With them, the words complicity
and understanding have been
true in every sense.
Yehudi Menuhin, at a rehearsal
for a concert held
on 26 April 1966,
to celebrate his fiftieth birthday
(22 April 1966.)

violin by Bach, Bartók, Prokofiev, and Hindemith among others are the exceptions which prove this rule, namely that the growing repertoire of sonatas for piano and violin, of concerti and of smaller works favors this combination of instruments. There are some concerti where the piano can—up to a point—replace the orchestra. But as in the case of concerti by Beethoven, Brahms, and Bartók this would be most unsatisfactory and unacceptable.

PIANISTS

*T*he function of the pianist who plays alongside the violinist has evolved over the generations. For a time concert announcements printed the violinist's name much more prominently than the pianist's. Sometimes the artist was described, somewhat curiously, as being "at the piano"—this despite the fact that the great sonatas are "for piano and violin." In the baroque era the piano was seen as subservient to the violin, although both instruments shared in the creative aspects of ornament and counterpoint. Gradually, however, the piano became a more powerful, dominant instrument. While the keyboard had once been mainly a tenderly percussive mechanism, as exemplified by the delicate clavichord, it has now been

*B*eginning in the eighteenth century, the violin repertoire was enriched by the appearance of more elaborate compositional forms, such as the sonata and the concerto. The instrument became more popular, and its collaboration with the harpsichord, bass, and other violins became more intricate. However, the performers were still often salon musicians, whose job was to brighten up the entertainments of high society, as in this charmingly floral scene. Despite their efforts, neither the violinist nor the harpsichordist seems able to cheer up the serious–faced spectator (their patron, perhaps) as he leans on the harpsichord. F. Falciatore, *Entertainment in a Park* (detail of musicians), eighteenth century. The Detroit Institute of Arts.

transformed into an all-purpose instrument, able to encompass harmonies, rhythms and melodies—all elements of orchestral scores in general, not to speak of the great electronic keyboards.

Today, beside a huge grand piano, the violin can easily be overshadowed. I tend to feel that the best era for the violin in this regard was the immediately post-Baroque period of early Beethoven, when the keyboard instruments were gentler and less aggressive—although in size the giant harpsichords of this era were even larger than the present concert grands.

I have had the great good fortune of playing music with my sister Hephzibah for nearly fifty years, from 1932 until her death in 1981. She was a wonderful pianist and companion, and over the years we played the entire sonata repertoire together, so

*F*rom a very early age
the fact that I was a violinist
meant that I had very close
relations with my partners,
particularly with the pianists.
Every day I would have
to work with a pianist
on the season's repertoire
(sonatas, concertos).
During those years, it often
happened that we would
be playing in small towns
that had no orchestra,
so we would include a concerto
with the piano substituting
for the orchestra.
Yehudi Menuhin in 1929,
with Hubert Giesen at the piano.

France), and our first concert at the Pleyel concert hall in 1934, we went on to do a large number of tours, concerts, and recordings together (including the Beethoven sonatas), despite the initial reservations of our mother. There is only one other person with whom I have ever managed to find a comparable balance and intimacy: my son Jeremy. We have given many concerts together, and today I still often accompany him with the baton.

I feel as if God has blessed me, by giving me a sister, and then a son, with whom I have been able to share my passion and my vision of music. And, in a general sense, each of my collaborations with pianists has been not only a source of musical enrichment, but above all a human experience. They have given rhythm to my days and my travels, because, unlike a pianist, a violinist who sets off on tour never travels alone. The spirit of a violinist, who only makes music with others, is fundamentally and intrinsically communitarian: life unfolds in an extended dialogue with other musicians.

I have spent my whole life as a violinist traveling with pianists. First with my teacher, Louis Persinger, who played wonderfully and who accompanied me on my first tour from October 1928 to March 1929. He was also an excellent chess player, and we enjoyed many games together on longer train journeys. At that time, our program included Brahms' *Sonata in D minor*. My first accompanist was Hubert Giesen, a young German who had been recommended by Adolf Busch—the idea of my 11-year-old sister playing with me, then aged 13, occurred to no one. Giesen was a very fine musician, a product of post-World War I Germany, a very special generation

completely attuned were we to one another. She was just thirteen when we discovered, under the aegis of Enesco, that our confederacy as brother and sister was matched by an incredible musical compatibility. Even without looking at each other, when we played together we could intuit each other's feelings and intentions. After our first recording (Mozart's *Sonata in A*, which won us the Record of the Year prize in

*P*ablo Casals had the stubbornness, the pride, and the steadfast character of the high Pyrenees that overlook Prades, the small Catalan town where he found refuge after Franco seized power. Resolutely faithful to his convictions, he then left Spain, never to return, and died in exile in Puerto Rico in 1973. For Spanish patriots and exiles he was a true prophet. For my part, I remember the great pleasure I had from the chamber music we shared at the Prades Festival and in Puerto Rico. Enesco apart, I never met anyone who was such a source of inspiration. With the precision of a watchmaker, with his extraordinary sense of musical impulse, Casals inspired those around him with an almost bodily feel for the rhythm and dynamics of a phrase.

marked by the first major upheaval in the young history of that nation.

I met Artur Balsam in Berlin, where he was studying at the Conservatory. Artur was a Polish Jew, and we used to speak German together. Although barely twenty years old he was already one of the great pianist–accompanists. I remember that he was never to be seen without some miniature score he was studying. He later became pianist with the New York Philharmonic, and died only very recently in United States.

When Artur left us, we brought a Belgian pianist into the family—Marcel Gazelle, who, like my sister, had worked with Marcel Ciampi. I was to work together with Marcel Gazelle for many long years; it was with him that I opened my school and he was its

Chamber music is music's ultimate expression, achieving the most perfect union and the most subtle balance between each of the different voices—which explains why it is such an inexhaustible source of satisfaction, as much for musicians as for listeners. I would be very happy if one day people's interest in music and advances in teaching meant that small amateur music groups sprang up all over the place, as was previously the case. In that way the courtesy, harmony, and exchange so fundamental to chamber work might find a voice that could be heard in our society. A rehearsal before the recording of the Tchaikovsky *Trio*, in 1936, Paris. We see Georges Enesco on my left, offering precious advice, Hephzibah on the piano, and Eisenberg on the cello.

director during the last years of his life. Marcel was an exceptional person, and for me he occupied the role of elder brother. He married my childhood friend, the violinist Jacqueline Salomons, who had also been a pupil of Enesco, and by this means he forged a further bond between us.

During World War II, Marcel lived in London, where he had joined the Belgian Free Forces, so I had to find a new partner. He was Adolphe Baller, whom I met in New York in 1939. Like Artur Balsam, he was a Polish-born Jew, and he had studied piano in Vienna with Theodor Leschetizky. After the cruel treatment to which the Nazis subjected him at the time of the *Anschluss* (they broke his fingers; fortunately, thanks to a wonderful doctor, his use of them was restored), he and his wife had taken refuge in the United States. They both came to live with us in California. Those years of collaboration, of shared life and communality,

leave me with many moving memories. We studied and worked together on so much music, particularly contemporary works: it was with Adolph that I chose the two Bartók works for my repertoire in the 1943 season. We traveled across all of America, from Alaska to Mexico, via Honolulu, but never to Europe, where war was raging. Together, we gave many concerts for audiences of music-lovers, and we also played a lot for soldiers. When Adolph founded a trio, with the

Hungarian Gabor Rejto on cello and the excellent Roman Totenberg on violin, he gave it the name "Alma" (which means "soul" in Spanish), after the name of our house and address in California. After the war, I no longer used a regular accompanist, although Marcel Gazelle and Adolph Baller remained very close friends.

I also recorded the Beethoven sonatas with Wilhelm Kempff, of whom one might say that he spent

More than any other conductor, Bruno Walter had an innate sense of accompaniment. He knew how to listen, understand, and put the soloists at ease. He was a man of infinite gentleness, and was eminently capable of blending and shaping the voice of an orchestra to match the inspiration and inflections of any soloist. Here he accompanies Josef Szigeti in a recording of a Beethoven concerto.

This Hungarian-born violinist was quite the opposite of Walter—a constructed musician, an intellectual in his way, who set great store by analysis and theory. He played in the old traditional style, holding the bow very close to his body, and practicing in this antiquated mode, which obliged the poor victim to play while holding a book under the right arm without letting it drop.

◆

his life with the composer—not only the music but also with the man himself. I could well imagine Beethoven saying to Wilhelm: "That's fine, Wilhelm, take any liberties you wish, you'll always be right"—and Wilhelm always was! Louis Kentner, who became my brother-in-law when he married Diana's sister, is a Hungarian with whom I played extensively and performed the cycle of Beethoven sonatas in London, Paris and New York.

The English accompanists who brought me wonderful support and understanding were Ivor Newton, a very elegant performer, and Gerald Moore, a large and warm-hearted man with thick fingers, who

played more delicately than one could ever imagine. Both were a source of joy in our musical partnerships. I love the Russian pianist Viktoria Postnikova, wife of the great conductor Gennady Rodjesvenski. She embraces the keyboard in one fell swoop, and has a power and thrust which matches Bartók, Beethoven and all the other works we performed together in Moscow and Paris. A fellow countryman of hers, Vladimir Ashkenazy, not only an outstanding pianist but a very fine conductor, displayed his people's proverbial generosity when he gave a concert with me for the benefit of my school.

No account of my companions in arms would be complete without that inspired artist Glenn Gould. Glenn was certainly the most original and creative pianist I could imagine playing with. He brought an altogether personal approach to everything he did while displaying an unbelievable command of the keyboard, its dynamics and timing. He was also a man with great depths of knowledge: he knew all the works of Alban Berg and Schönberg from memory, and was himself a wonderful writer and literary connoisseur. In addition he was a composer, and an excellent piece for string quartet and other works provide testimony to his creative talent.

I have also played and recorded with outstanding harpsichordists: first in New York with Wanda Landowska, who had rescued the harpsichord from categorization as a museum instrument, restoring it to its present authentic and dominant position in Baroque music. She is a characterful Pole who carries her Baroque sensibilities to the extreme. She also has a strong gift for improvisation which marks many harpsichord players. In George Malcolm, England has an outstanding harpsichordist with whom I recorded Bach, Handel, and other Baroque works.

Finally I should not forget the music I created with my teacher Enesco. He was a great pianist and an inspiration, and although we did not play together in public, I fondly remember studying the many works of the sonata repertoire with him.

CONDUCTORS

*W*hile the violinist and the pianist form a one-to-one relationship, a conductor is not necessarily a born accompanist. Ideally both conductor and orchestra are convinced of the soloist's interpretation, and a wonderful symbiosis ensues. Otherwise the whole can literally fall into many parts. Worst of all is a situation where the conductor is completely inimical to the soloist's interpretation and manner, or vice versa. I always feel that it is important to make music, not discuss theory, and in any case musicians much prefer a minimum of words and a maximum of actual playing. Convention dictates that the conductor accompanies the soloist, yet sensitive performers will adjust especially if there is much to learn from either conductor or soloist. Incompatibilities can occur, as among any human beings, but if both soloist and conductor are on their best behavior they can usually survive the evening—if no more!

I have never had any problems—except on two occasions. Once I had to play the Mendelssohn and Tchaikovsky concerti with a conductor who seemed to have only one metronome tempo, as if from birth he had been committed to one pulse and knew no other. It all fell apart at a certain point—entirely my fault—as

*I*t is difficult to imagine a more careful arrangement. The architecture of this orchestra bears the stamp of the person conducting it: Herbert von Karajan. As in this picture, Karajan was a person who left nothing to chance. Everything, down to the last details of his physical appearance, was calculated. He often conducted with his eyes closed: this expressed, of course, the intensity of his concentration, but this went hand in hand with a certain affectation. Illness would profoundly transform him, and one might say that through this suffering he became a very great conductor. The Berlin Philharmonic, conducted by Herbert von Karajan, 1967.

*T*he baton, the attribute
and supreme symbol
of the conductor, is nothing more
than a curious bit of wood one
can very well do without. In fact,
without a baton the conductor's
hands become more expressive.
Pierre Boulez is a good example
of the eloquence of the bare
gesture. He never conducts
with a baton, even
in the Wagnerian repertoire,
which requires huge ensembles.
One wonders whether the baton
might be an offspring of the violin
bow. Originally, in small ensembles,
it was the first violin who
conducted the other musicians
from his seat. In the seventeenth
century, in large ensembles,
a baton was used to beat the
measure by tapping on the floor.
In the eighteenth century,
a roll of paper gave the signal.
Finally, in the nineteenth century,
the conductor's baton appeared—
probably a memory
of the bow used by the first violin.
Certainly the use of a baton which
magnifies the gestures is easier
for a large orchestra to follow.
Zubin Mehta conducting
the New York Philharmonic.

FLAMMARION · L'images des images · Archi · SIGN. 16

I had taken one of those fateful Greek oaths, that after the last four-bar *tutti* at the coda of the Mendelssohn concerto, I would play at my own speed regardless. I finished the concert along with a few other first desks—about eight bars ahead of the rest. Unfortunately the same cleavage occurred in the audience, some of whom applauded when I finished, and the rest clapped as the orchestra brought up the rear, and stopped. My only other problem as a soloist was with a great musician who treated the orchestra with an intolerable high-handedness which I found insulting

to their dignity. I made it clear that I was on the side of the orchestra and resolved never to play with that conductor again.

The very first conductor I knew was Alfred Hertz, an excellent German conductor, who was the permanent "musical director" (as they are now called) of the San Francisco Symphony. We currently live in an age of constant motion, change and with a desire for variety and adventure. Thus the conductor who remains all his life with one orchestra, as was the case until fifty years ago, no longer exists. The audience

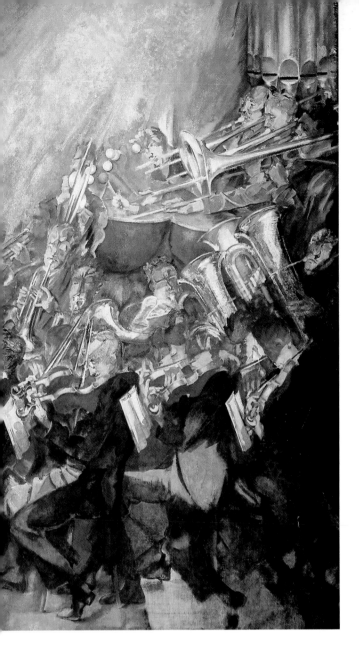

We know Mahler the composer, but his activities as a conductor and his efforts to make the music of his contemporaries better known are also part of the history of music. Glorious were the years when he conducted at the Vienna Opera, despite the cabals intriguing against him. This picture of Mahler gives the measure of his spirit and his commitment as an artist. He was so much a part of the music that here, in an imaginative and visionary representation, the painter places him in the middle of the orchestra, as if at the center of the musical whirlwind of which he is the source. On his lectern there is no score; he was presumably conducting from memory.

Max Oppenheimer (1885–1954), *The Orchestra*, 1935. Vienna, Österreichische Galerie.

---

wants variety and often the conductor wants to be musical director of as many orchestras as he can, giving each the minimum required to retain his title—about three is the maximum anyone has ever achieved. As far as I know there is no prize for this kind of competitiveness. At the age of three I heard Alfred Hertz conducting his orchestra—the first Mozart symphony, Brahms, Wagner, Beethoven (the repertoire was of course overwhelmingly German and Austrian, and contemporary music hardly existed.) Exotic musics were unheard of and even Debussy had not entered the hallowed circle of Beethoven with a little Tchaikovsky. Thus the first orchestral works I played was the Tchaikovsky Concerto and the Lalo *Symphonie espagnole*.

Since then I have known virtually all the conductors although I almost missed George Szell, with whom I was to play in Cleveland. As a married man with four children I had managed to catch chicken pox from one of them in London and was forced to cancel the concert. He invited me, however, some time later to conduct his orchestra, and it was an exhilarating experience to work with impeccably drilled musicians and to allow them for once to relax. He was reputedly a hard taskmaster and a great many of his musicians had sought the care of a particular psychiatrist I knew who had moved from Boston to Cleveland!

The first conductors who knew me as more than an infant were Paul Paray in Paris, when I was eleven and Bruno Walter in Berlin, when I was thirteen. I knew Paray from his first invitation to me to play concerti in Paris in 1927, until his death: we played our last concerti together shortly before he died in Monte Carlo in 1979. Other great conductors appeared in the course of my concert tours and included Toscanini and Koussevitzky and the great English conductors, Sir John Barbirolli, Sir Adrian Boult, Sir Malcolm Sargent, Sir Charles Groves, and many others. My early recordings in Paris were all with Enesco or Pierre Monteux.

The outstanding conductors were those with whom I recorded, who inspired me, and who were much more than just timekeepers. Georges Enesco, for example, was a conductor for whom any orchestra would give of its best, playing for him twice as well as usually; Furtwängler embodied the noble German Romantic tradition; Elgar was both a great conductor and a fine composer. These were all musicians of another dimension. There is hardly a conductor since Karl Muck, who had been the conductor of the Berlin Symphony Orchestra in the first years of World War I, from Sir Georg Solti, until the present generation of Zubin Mehta, Sir Simon Rattle, Colin Manzel, and Claudio Abbado, with whom I have not worked at one time or another.

However, for me the most compassionate conductor, who as an accompanist felt almost physically

*S*travinsky was a kind of Picasso of music, capable of composing in all styles, and of adapting to the requirements of all genres. Whether the inspiration was Neoclassical, serial, folk, contrapuntal, polytonal, opera, ballet, or symphony, he was equally at home. Nothing disturbed him, and he remained master of himself in all circumstances. A special light illuminated his music and his thinking, making him a man devoid of veils and mystery. All his scores reflect this clarity of musical and human spirit. They are transparent, easy to read, and they have the intelligibility characteristic of works of genius. One of my great regrets is that we never had the opportunity to record his *Violin Concerto* together as Stravinsky desired.

with the soloist, was Bruno Walter. With Bruno Walter, my career took on a new dimension. This was in 1929. I was not yet thirteen and I was playing in Berlin, the musical capital of the West, the city with the most prestigious orchestras, the best conductors, and the most discerning audiences. On the program we had the "three B's"—in other words, concerti by Bach, Beethoven, and Brahms. In the concert hall were such notables as Fritz Kreisler, Bronislav Gimpel, Carl Flesch, and Albert Einstein. At the end of the concert, which was a veritable triumph, Einstein complimented me to a rather disproportionate extent. Needless to say, moments like this are not easily forgotten, but the main thing I remember from the experience is

We know Haydn's marvelous
quartets, but we rarely think
of him performing his own music.
Here we see him engaged
in precisely that instructive
exercise. He has chosen
to take the viola part, so as to
place himself in the midst
of the harmony, at the heart
of the quartet's music, listening
to the voices of the first
and second violins,
while the cello provides
the harmonic foundation
of the edifice. Like Haydn,
Enesco also enjoyed playing
the viola, because it gave him
a central musical perspective.
Joseph Haydn Playing
with a Quartet.
Vienna, City Museum.

what Bruno Walter gave me, as a human being and as a musician: his lack of dogmatism, his compassion, his constant references to the human voice, which was what guided his conception of music, and the spirit he breathed into his music.

The least metronomic, the least "sergeant-major"-like conductor was Wilhelm Furtwängler (1886–1954) who felt that the work he was conducting was a section of living time and that he was a boat he

was guiding, carried along by the stream. He would no more dictate than he could ask the waters to stop: the work itself dictated the speed, its rate of flow, the breadth of the river or the rapids over which he must go. The Beethoven concerto I played with him in 1947, which we recorded a few years later, was one of my finest experiences, and one of the most intense from every point of view. The madness of the war engulfed Furtwängler in a controversy, as he remained in Germany. People were unwilling to recognize that, although he remained in Germany, he had refused to compromise and had incurred the hostility of the Nazi régime. It was a long time before some Jewish people could open their minds and hearts to Furtwängler, despite the reconciliatory power of his music.

THE QUARTET

There is no doubt in my mind that the highest form of music making is the string quartet. The two women's voices, soprano and contralto, harmonize completely with the two men's voices of tenor or baritone and bass. The quality of listening, the quality of "team work", of adjusting to one another, of recognizing the main voice wherever it may be, of reconciling the different accents and inflections, and the purity of the intonation, is unequalled by any other ensemble, except perhaps human voices themselves. The repertoire has always demanded the highest concepts from the composer. String quartets cannot but represent the noblest features of musical creation. Every emotion is sublimated and the whole range of musical styles is covered in the quartets from Haydn to Bartók and beyond.

The quartet is the purest, most complete, and most noble genre of Western music. It was with Haydn and above all Mozart that it came of age. Previously, there had been many possible instrumental combinations, but in the course of the eighteenth century the joining of these four voices in harmony enjoyed unprecedented success. The popularity of the quartet was due to the presence of a large number of amateur musicians in Viennese high society who needed a repertoire they could play in their salons. Thus the quartet, which demands the greatest courtesy among partners, was born. Italy, the land of virtuosi, gave birth to the concerto and the opera. Austria gave birth to the quartet, and the genre made it possible for composers to reach the pinnacle of their art. Beethoven, the Romantics, Ravel, and Bartók all turned their talent to the quartet, merging the greatest economy of means with the greatest depths of emotion.

There is no better school for learning style, whether of genre, place, person or period, than quartet playing. It is the principal bearer of musical formation at my school at Stoke d'Abernon, and at the other three schools patterned after mine in Madrid (the Escuela Superior de Musica Reina Sofia, led by Paloma O'Shea), Grenoble (led by Clothilde Munch, a niece of Charles Munch the great conductor) and the David Oistrakh School at Ingolstadt near Munich. At Stoke d'Abernon—and by implication at the other schools too—there are eleven quartets drawn from forty students, including players as young as nine years old.

A mon bien cher confrère et ami J. Chaplain

In this painting by Hieronymus Bosch, human beings are dominated by an ear. An anonymous crowd creeps along, crushed and enslaved by a monstrous earlobe. Interestingly, the arrow pierces this ear at a point which, according to acupuncturists, corresponds to the most sensitive parts of our anatomy. We know that hearing is the most immediate and most intense of the senses, and therefore the sense which renders people most vulnerable. But, by the opposite token, it can also give supreme pleasure and confer magic powers. At left we see the legendary Greek poet Arion escaping from his attackers by summoning up dolphins whom he has enchanted with his music and who carry him safely away. Gustave Moreau (1826–1898), *Arion*, 1891. Paris, Musée du Petit Palais. Hieronymus Bosch (c. 1450–c. 1516), *The Garden of Earthly Delights* (detail of Hell). Madrid, Museo del Prado.

LISTENING

Music, indeed all artistic creation and all craftsmanship, is a sublimation of our emotional and intellectual capacities which often have no outlet, may find the wrong one, or remain imprisoned within the self. I truly believe that music and the other arts which have their source in the realm of the senses, can exercise a great influence on the way a human being grows, and can also affect the values and ethical assumptions of a society which is too often influenced by judgments born of frustration, prejudice, and the baser motives of revenge and punishment. We must therefore learn how to use our senses in the most positive way.

Noise is now becoming
intolerable, all the more
so when it has no meaning.
It has lost its signal value,
and retains only its power
of aggression.
We no longer hear nature telling
us what kind of weather
to expect because of the machines
that are invading our lives
and alienating us.
Earthbound noises were already
quite enough; now we also
have to put up with noise
from the sky.
The roar of aircraft is added
to the din of cars, to deafen us
and destroy the silence that is
so necessary to our existence.
Jet above Hong Kong.

listener's hearing capacity. The escalation of decibels is destroying our capacity to hear.

Thus if hearing is a faculty that affects us deeply, it may also become a threat, exposing us to danger. Nevertheless, our hearing remains first and foremost a source of joy and emotional richness, and music is the privileged agent of this phenomenon. We would like to think of it, after all, as our first communicating sense. We are always being swept along by flows of emotion—sadness, happiness, desire, and so on. If we witness a happy event we feel happiness, while the sight of misfortune makes us sad (at least we can hope this is the general reaction!) This is what is called sympathy—in the proper sense of the term, from the Greek *syn* (with) and *pathos* (feeling), and is the basis of compassion—in other words, rapport, correspondence, and a sharing of emotions. Music awakens in us a kind of communication: we vibrate in sympathetic resonance with it, like musical intervals, like the fifths and octaves that are the multiples of vibrations. One emotion stirs a reciprocal emotion, in the same way that one vibration stirs its correspondent.

Nature itself sometimes provides an image of its inherent universal harmony. Several years ago, I was in Mykonos, Greece, in early spring. In the middle of the bay, there is an island, uninhabited save for a

*E*verything in the lives of these bees is predetermined. Every moment, every function, every action obeys the genetic code proper to their species. It is astonishing that the human race, which gradually succeeded in freeing itself from genetics, then felt the need to replace this determination by another, which embraces every element of life. I refer to theocracy, which, with its rules, codes, and prohibitions, determines and constrains humans, who then allow superior powers to make decisions for them, or simply to bless the very folly they will commit anyway. Honeybees gathering nectar from a tansy.

chapel perched on the peak, with its back to a precipice tumbling down to the sea. I was walking on earth that was still damp, and strewn with a mass of colored flowers so numerous and dense that there was hardly an inch unembroidered by flowers. It was like a richly decorated Oriental carpet, soft and alive. However, the most extraordinary thing was not the feast of colors, but the concert that nature was giving at that moment. The flowers had attracted a massive presence of bees, who were visiting blossom after blossom to gather pollen. When I stopped to listen to the intoxicating hum of their activity, all of a sudden I realized that it was not at all a confused, disordered noise, but rather a secret harmony of creation: the bees were giving out two notes, and, what is more, those two notes formed the interval of a fifth. The larger bees were giving the lower tone and a smaller sized bee was producing the upper tone—it was a true symbiosis of the two subspecies, establishing compatibility through the strongest of all intervals, the fifth.

I have no idea how to analyze this wonder of nature. But it seems that the search for the fifth is one of the primal necessities of the universe. We emit and receive vibrations, which follow a secret order and underlying harmony. Some would even say that the intervals between the planets—the distances separating them from one another—correspond closely to the intervals of music, so that fifths, thirds, and octaves become simply the musical images of these celestial intervals.

This idea is as disturbing as it is seductive, and on a couple of occasions I was able to experience it for myself. The first time I heard it was on a trip to Russia in the 1970s for the biannual meeting of the UNESCO International Music Council, of which I was then president. The Russians were presenting a display of folk music during which a Mongolian peasant who no doubt represented the folk tradition from which Tibetan monks draw their technique, began to sing. The musicians gathered could hardly believe what they had heard. This astonishing technique depends on the control of the overtones which can be sounded separately while the ground tone is not heard. Usually it is the other way around: we hear the fundamental and the overtones are added, and the keyboard vibrates with sympathetic strings. But here this Mongolian peasant could extract the overtones and ignore the fundamental.

CULTURAL HABITS

We live in a world which gives pride of place to sight, and where hearing takes second place. The image is everything. However, among African tribes knowledge comes first through the ear. To grasp the reality of an object, they knock it to make it resonate, and then listen to the vibrations to determine whether it will be beneficial or harmful.

Some people still have this sense of things, and they speak of the vibrations transmitted to them by a

place, or by someone's voice. In general, however, we judge the world with our eyes: we buy fruit because it is big and colorful. What dictates our choice is the color of an apricot, the satiny look of a peach, or the red of an apple, even though the taste rarely matches the visual promise. A piece of cloth, a shoe, or a chair only really reveal themselves to us if we touch them. It is through physical contact that we are able to judge things and evaluate them. The eye, and through it our sense of touch, seeks to dominate and thus we live our life by

Men at prayer look much
the same anywhere
in the world.
These Tibetan monks could
as well be Christian monks,
wrapped in their thoughts
while raising their spirits
in communication
with the divine.

The harmonic form of singing
sometimes used by Tibetan
monks is one of the most
astonishing ways of entering
into transcendence
and of reproducing the music
of the spheres.
Monks in the Temple of Jokhang.
Tibet, Lhasa.

means of intermediaries. The world ends up like a giant
living advertisement, because what we see is the realm
of appearance, and therefore, quite possibly, of dissimu-
lation. The eye dominates us, but it can also fool us.

Music, on the other hand, cannot deceive,
because it belongs to the real and is transmitted to us
by direct contact. It derives from being and not from
appearance. I would add that music can act on being
and transform it. In the same way that an Indian's flute

*O*rpheus is a splendid symbol

of the beneficial power

of music and its capacity

to transform those who hear it.

When Orpheus sings,

accompanying himself on his lyre,

people and animals,

as well as trees and rocks

fall under his spell.

He has the power to soothe

the waves of the sea and to put

serpents to sleep.

He even moves the fearsome gods

of Hades after the death

of Eurydice, and wins himself

the right to search for his beloved

beyond the waters of the Styx.

Nicolas Poussin (1594–1665),

Landscape with Orpheus

and Eurydice.

Paris, Musée du Louvre.

In today's world, music and dance are truly antidotes to violence. Since September 1994, with the support of the European Community Commission and UNESCO, I have established a project called MUS-E designed to introduce into primary education a form of teaching based on music, song, and dance, in order to channel the energy of children living in difficult environments. Very recently the ministries of education in Spain and Portugal have signed a protocol with my foundation to introduce this program in their countries. Perhaps by the time this book is published other countries will have followed suit. The stabilizing potential of music and body movement, the calm and concentration they produce, are spectacular and objective facts. Every day we are seeing the results of this work in several European countries. I cannot understand why, faced with this evidence, governments do not set up programs like this in all schools. There can be no better way of assuring the mental health of our society and a greater harmony among all humankind.

can charm the most fearsome snake and tame its murderous instinct, music can modify an individual's inner world: Tamino with his magic flute, soothing wild animals; Orpheus, who moves inanimate objects and charms even the gods of Hades; or the Pied Piper of Hamelin, whose flute seduces all the town's rats—all these are eloquent representations of the magical power of music.

These phenomena are well known to people who practice music therapy. Bach chorales no less than folk music are capable of healing, soothing, and developing the potential of those who listen to them. I have had occasion to observe these almost miraculous results in recent months, thanks to the MUS-E project (Music, source of Equilibrium and tolerance), which I set up with the support of the European Community

Commission and UNESCO, under the aegis of the International Yehudi Menuhin Foundation. The aim of the project is to introduce song and dance into the curricula of "difficult" primary schools. In France, Belgium, Switzerland, Hungary, Estonia, England, Spain, Portugal, and Germany, children have thus been given a chance to develop their listening and aural capacities. For them, this contact with music is a stabilizing force, even if it is only for a few hours a week. The children's personalities, their sensory development, their ability to find their place within a group of fellow human beings, their capacity for improvisation and creation, their memory, and their studies—all these blossom astonishingly during these programs. It is as if the children are reshaped by the vibrations, and mistrust, prejudice, fear, and violence disappear from the classroom.

Ever since the invention

of the musical bow,

since that first tenuous sound

was obtained by rubbing

the animal hair strings and bows

against each other (right),

humankind has instinctively

developed all kinds of techniques

to enrich the color

and power of the instrument.

The Indian *sarangi* (left)

is a member of the string family,

at once both rustic

and extraordinarily complex,

for while it only has three bowed

strings of thick gut, by way

of compensation it has a large

number of resonating metal

strings evidenced by the forest

of pegs on the side, situated

below the melody strings,

which vibrate in a kind

of sound halo that is both

disturbing and enchanting.

I love the face of this player—it

has a kind of attentive innocence

as if he too were only a medium

rather than a prime mover.

A musician from Jaisalmer.

Rajasthan, Thar Desert.

*M*usical bow from Argentina.

Paris, Musée de l'Homme.

VIOLINS OF THE WORLD

*I*t is striking how different stringed instruments from different cultures seem to carry not only the imprint of the culture's visual style but also the aural imprint of its language and manners of speech. The contrast between the Peking fiddle with its two strings and somewhat nasal inflection and a melodic Italian instrument is very noticeable. Yet whatever forms the instruments may take and the type of people who use these instruments to express feelings, a basic continuity of sound remains as a particular characteristic of the violin.

The violin by its nature brings a melodic quality to peoples and languages that may be rougher and

*T*he person who made these *sokous* is an African brother of the great violin makers of Cremona. He was not working with the fir found in the forests of Italy, but with local wood for the sound box and goatskin for the sound board, because these were the materials at hand. This man, who is at once instrument maker, musician, astrologer, and poet, belongs to the caste of people known as *griots*, the oral historians of the tribe who knows the stories of all the wars fought, property lines, marriages and deaths. He is always listened to and regularly sings the history of his people, improvising as he goes along. Against the stone wall are instruments in various stages of manufacture. All that is needed now is the addition of the horsehair string, which will be made to vibrate with the horsehair strings of a curved bow. *Sokous* by the *griot*, Tiemogo Koïta. Burkina Faso, 1990.

more disjointed than the music the instrument itself produces. In melody it is the subtlest of inflections between notes, the distribution of time over a melodic phrase, the notes that need a little more or less stress, the phrase that rises or falls—these are elements of subtlety which the violin player must know and feel. In every case, therefore, there is a response to the finest degrees of calibration.

No stringed instrument, least of all the violin, can be a crude affair. The crudest—if one would wish to designate them so—are those which tune their lower strings to a drone. And yet even this music, as I know from experience, has subtle complications which are almost inimitable by any except the genuine native players.

This violin is cut from
a single piece of wood.
Like most of the bowed
instruments found in the ancient
Americas, it is a solid object,
with a short neck
and one single string.
The Apaches manufactured
similar instruments,
using hollowed-out cactus,
while the Cubans used bamboo.
The highly curved bow
inescapably evokes its origins
in the hunting bow.
A single-string Argentinian violin.
Paris, Musée de l'Homme.

COUSINS OF THE VIOLIN

Based on the principle of a sound box, strings and a bow, the most weird, unlikely and beautiful instruments have been devised in response to the esthetic norms of the particular culture, to the materials available, and the use they could be put to. Gourds serve as sound boxes for many Africans, coconuts for the Chinese, and tortoiseshells for Celtic musicians. Animal hair and in the case of the Mongols very rough horsehair, tightened and held by the bow, create the friction required to set the string vibrating. One can readily imagine giving this recipe to a group of children from heterogeneous backgrounds. Presented with all kinds of materials and tools, each child would make an instrument using their ingenuity, fantasy, and sense of structure, and the result would be as many different instruments as different children.

The first time I saw a Chinese fiddle was during the early 1940s at a military airfield in Arizona, where

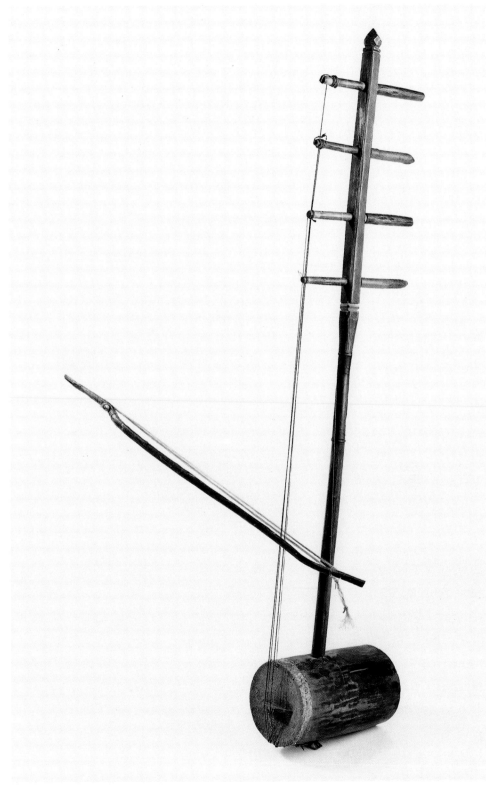

*U*nlike the Western violin,

which is supported horizontally

against the collarbone

and by the arms, the Chinese

violin is played vertically,

with the sound box resting

on the instrumentalist's thigh.

Despite its apparent simplicity,

the musical and technical

possibilities of the Chinese violin

are infinite.

The first time I heard

the astonishing sound

of this instrument was at

a military airfield in Arizona,

during World War II.

In China, musical instruments

are classified according

to their principal material.

String instruments thus belong

to the silk category,

because their strings are made

of silk—which explains the soft,

satiny, mellow quality

of the Chinese violin.

Chinese four-stringed violin.

Paris, Musée de l'Homme.

the Americans were training Chinese pilots. These young men brought this instrument with them to remind them of their hauntingly beautiful music. The horsehair of the bow passes between the two strings, and thus the violinist need never lose his bow, which can play each string separately or both simultaneously.

The violin rests on the knees of the seated player and the special techniques used are *glissando* and *vibrato*. The sound box may be cylindrical, hexagonal or octagonal, can vary in size, and it can be decorated with lizard or snakeskin. The bridge is of wood or bone, and the two or more strings are of silk. The Chinese are very proud that their modern fiddle is improved and makes a louder sound: the bow is no longer attached to the strings but can be separated from the instrument. I once heard the most beautiful performance by a Chinese girl at the Beijing Conservatoryof Music, where, as at Chinese medical schools, the educational traditions are both Chinese and Western in equal measure.

India too boasts its own stringed instrument. Bearing little resemblance to any other instrument the *sarangi* is very large, bulbous and has as many as thirty-five sympathetic metal strings that shore up the sound and the notes of the three or four thick gut strings which are played with the bow. It produces a beautiful sound and a great player can use it to convey poetry and infinite beauty. Certainly a rural, perhaps even a nomadic instrument, the *sarangi* follows the goats and shepherds in the search for new pastures.

The Senegalese have a very small violin with four strings, and the sound box is made of an

The player seems quite detached from his instrument. It is big and clumsy and the bow is thick and heavy. But he listens intently to the music he is making. The faces of musicians as they play are quite fascinating—sometimes they are a part of the music, at other times they appear detached. It is wonderful that finally we have come to appreciate the musical cultures and arts of India. It is thanks to such passionate musicologists as Alain Daniélou that we now have an understanding and respect for these sophisticated and fascinating arts.

Sarangi player. Jodhpur, India.

*H*ere we have another musical bow (left). This time it is not the player's mouth that serves as the sound box, but a small container fitted to one end of the instrument. What is astonishing and unusual is that the musician holds his instrument horizontally, almost like an Italian violin. Once again we note the difference between the expression of the "violinist," who is relaxing into the reverie of an improvised melody, and the attentive drummer, who watches as he accompanies. Senegal, musicians with a single string violin and gourd drums. The people of North Africa also have instruments with bowed strings. Here (right) a Berber plays a rebab: the pressure of his fingers on the single string determine the pitch of the sound, and his curved bow sets the string vibrating. The Berbers were a great civilization who ruled a very large part of North Africa around 5,000 years ago.

armadillo shell with iguana or lizard skin stretched over the hollow. The bow, also of horsehair, is a rudimentary curved stick. The experienced fiddler can draw excellent sounds and rhythms from this instrument, which when I tried to play it refused any kind of cooperation!

Among the other cousins of the violin are the South American violins made of hollowed-out bamboo; the Persian *kemancha* or *kamanche*, where half of a coconut stretched with sheepskin serves as a sound box; the Mongols' *morin-khuur*, with a square body and carved horse's head on top; and the Bulgarian *gadulka*, which is held vertically on the knee. Civilizations entirely unknown to each other somehow created instruments that were at once similar and dissimilar. Since the dawn of time, these civilizations have been

*T*he Bulgarian *gadulka*

is an heir of the medieval rebec,

from which it derives

its pear-shaped profile.

Equipped with a number

of resonating strings,

it is generally played vertically,

with the instrument resting

on the knee. This is a beautiful

photograph of the delight which

music can create. I have rarely

seen even a violinist graduating

from a conservatory looking

as radiant as this.

Bulgaria, Pernik Festival, 1980.

in unknowing communion, celebrating a universal sonority and searching for a voice at once collective and individual.

THE VIOLIN'S ROLE IN THE WORLD

*I*n this proliferation of forms it was the evolution of the European violin—perhaps the Italian, East European and Russian folk instruments—which culminated in the first Gaspar da Salo and the Maggini. These instruments came into use ahead of the Amati family who reduced fairly large instruments to a convenient size and ultimately launched the modern violin. The "parent" instruments have an extraordinary deep, ecclesiastical sound, far more moving than the later instruments even of Stradivarius and Guarnieri. The character of these early violins is inspired by the religious period of the Middle Ages: while the Stradivarius belongs to the salon and concert hall society, the Maggini belongs to the church. This Italian violin became the model for what the whole world recognizes as a violin—far and away more practical than others.

Thus the Indians who came into contact with Western traditions adopted the violin, an instrument more flexible, more versatile than the *sarangi*. However Indians play the violin in their own way, sitting cross-legged on the floor. In this way the left hand is free to emulate the particular style of singing which requires wide *glissandi* and fluctuations at various speeds with unfailing accuracy of pitch and speed, thus imitating the undulations of the human voice as used in India's classical music.

*H*ere we have one of the handsomest cousins of the violin: the *morin-khuur* of Mongolia. At the top of the neck it proudly displays a horse, the emblem of the Mongolian people, for it was on horseback that these nomads, under the leadership of Genghis Khan, conquered the world as far as Central Europe. It was in the thirteenth century that the *morin-khuur* first made its appearance in the Mongol court, with a trapezoidal, almost square body, elegant neck, and two horsehair strings. It is held rather like a cello, resting on the floor at a slight angle, with the instrumentalist seated or squatting. The instrument is often richly decorated; the sound board shown here depicts a galloping horse. What could be more natural than a horsehair violin carried away on horseback to the ends of the world? In fact this is exactly the scene depicted on the flap of this book, in one of my favorite paintings by Myfanwy Pavelic.

Morin-khuur.

Paris, Musée de l'Homme.

*T*his fresco represents
Dhritarashtra, the king
of musician gods, playing the lute.
Similarly in the Western world
sacred figures such as Apollo
and King David are associated
with stringed instruments.
The Bible tells us that David played
the *kinnor*, a kind of violin,
to cure King Saul of his depression.
In our Judaeo-Christian world,
as in Islam and the Byzantine
musical rites, however,
music serves the words, enabling
them to be broadcast
far and wide, and allowing
more people to hear them.
This is the background
of Gregorian chant,
which exists to carry the words
and has little rhythmic definition.
Folk music, by contrast,
has much more melodic
and rhythmic definition
and the words count for less.
My prayer has always been
through music, rather than words.
Kham (Sichaun), Tibet,
fresco in the Sakya Monastery,
Laghon (seventh century).

As we know India
has adopted our Western violin,
and this innocently immodest
young lady plays her instrument
à l'indienne, with the head
of the violin resting almost
on the floor. Her position
indicates she could not possibly
be a real violinist.
The musician Lakshminarayan
Subramanian (right),
is one of India's most inspired
violinists, a great musician
and instrumentalist.
It was wonderful to see
uninitiated audiences in Europe
completely captivated
by his playing, and welcoming
him with ovations.

Most incredible of all is the extraordinary precision with which Indian musicians are capable of sliding rapidly and accurately between notes. Of course their hearing is more acute than ours inasmuch as they have never compromised with perfect fifths on a keyboard. An Indian wandering off the correct pitch would correct it instantly. Our ears are corrupt by comparison, for we constantly listen to the piano and to the distortion of the perfect fifth, but the violin has never had to compromise and is therefore particularly suited to Indian music. Another advantage a violin offers to Indian music is that with four strings it can be tuned to the different requirements of Indian scales. The violin, as we have seen, is particularly adapted to the use of *scordatura*—literally "out of tune"—which certain technical passages demand.

*W*e know from first hand experience that the Gypsy and the Jew took the violin with them on their peregrinations. Both are nomadic peoples: the Gypsy from India, the Jew from the Middle East, and both

*R*ather aptly for this book,
the famous photographer
who captured this moment,
Henri Cartier-Bresson,
sees hunting
with a bow as a metaphor
for the photographer's art.
In his view, the photographer
is like an archer, lying in wait
for his prey, and his camera
is a kind of bow that captures
the decisive moment on film.
Thus what we have here
is a photographer-archer framing
a view of a violinist-archer.
He is probably about to play
one of his country's folk tunes,
just as soon as he finds
a way out of this complicated
maneuver (how did he get
the violin and bow out
of his case, while holding
the latter on his forearm?).
Los Remedios,
near Mexico City.
Photograph by
Henri Cartier-Bresson.

found a kindred spirit in the violin, an easy companion to transport and a voice to sing their sorrows and delights.

The instrument also found new roots in the highlands of Scotland, Ireland and the mists of Norway. It could be used to accompany dance or song and for ceremonial purposes. These instruments belong to the open air as did the relatively primitive instruments of the Russian village, and they are often tuned differently from the classical instrument to convey this sense of space, sea and sky, E-A-E-A and E-A-D-A being common sequences.

In Scotland I once joined a group of local fiddlers and was amazed to hear how their often gnarled and clumsy fingers played accurately and in time, and with an infallible rhythm which accompanied the dancers in their reels. Scottish folk fiddlers play almost exclusively in the first position, and produce extraordinary added notes which defy anyone not born to such a technique. They never play out of tune or

Gypsies have a very personal
way of playing the violin.
The two violinists here are not
playing one of those fiendish
improvisations known
only to Gypsies—they are
probably accompanying a singer
(perhaps also a dancer),
because neither of them
is holding his violin in such
a way that he could play a melody
(most likely, they are playing
only the upbeat.)
The crowd behind them
is watching a spectacle
that we tantalizingly cannot see.
Czechoslovakia, 1966.
Photograph by Josef Koudelka.

rhythm, no matter how rapid the latter may be. The Scots have a wonderful ear for music—a better ear than we can develop living in our urban jungles.

TOWARDS AN INTERMINGLING OF CULTURES

I have always had the feeling that something vital was missing from my musical being: I was trained in the formal, literary, classical tradition. Improvisation had no place there, even though I have always regarded the violin as an instrument whose very essence is the making of sound at the very instant—that is, improvisation. The greatest musicians can convey the sense of improvisation, even when playing a classical work for the hundredth time. It is akin to the eagerness we feel when really hungry and longing for a particular dish which we then eat with the same sense of joy and immediate satisfaction each time. Unfortunately many classical players including

*I*t is hard to imagine
a folk music tradition richer
than that of the Celts,
whether in Ireland or in Scotland.
In the ancient Celtic civilization,
the king of instruments
was the harp.
Then other instruments
took over, among them
the bagpipes and the violin.
The playing of great Irish folk
fiddlers is full of arabesques
and convolutions that recall
the great stone crosses set
at crossroads in Ireland.
But in the country's pubs you
also find all manner of violinists
accompanying dancing
and popular song.
These players nevertheless
have an inborn sense
of rhythm and melody.
Reflection in a pub mirror.
Northern Ireland.

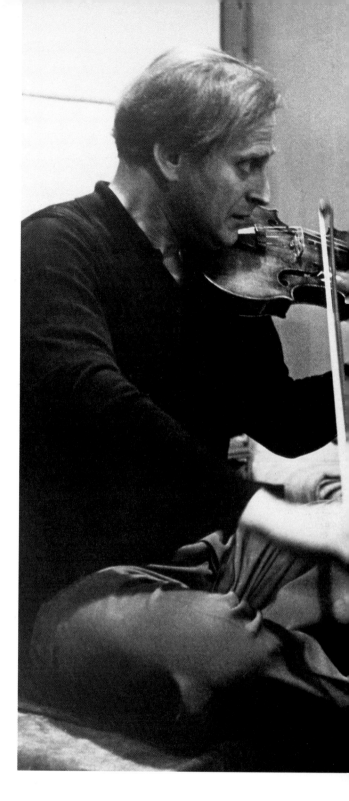

Ravi Shankar revealed to me a new dimension in music. It was thanks to him that I came to understand the religious quality of this art, and the devotion and inspiration which it demanded. In India, music is seen as an offering. But it is also the product of hard work and particularly intense experience, because Indian music demands a mastery and a level of imagination almost unknown to us in the West. Since the written score does not exist as intermediary, the Indian musician must be at once both performer and composer. Thus, before he can begin playing, he has to learn and assimilate a far stricter discipline than that of our classical tradition: he has to know hundreds of scales, with their infinite variations, and has to master the inexhaustible wealth of highly complex rhythmic combinations. The first time I heard Ravi Shankar play this music, which has neither beginning nor end, but which is fluid and moves like a river, I was astonished. For me, he is one of the world's greatest musicians. Yehudi Menuhin and Ravi Shankar.

orchestra musicians play with repletion, as if they had had enough of their particular dish.

I have been fortunate to meet two outstanding musicians in the art of improvisation. I encountered Ravi Shankar on our first visit to Delhi in 1952. Indian classical music, like Indian dance and thought, was a total revelation for me. It was extraordinary to enter into a world that has its own ways of expression, its own completely different forms and instruments. I was taken by Ravi Shankar's playing and found it to have

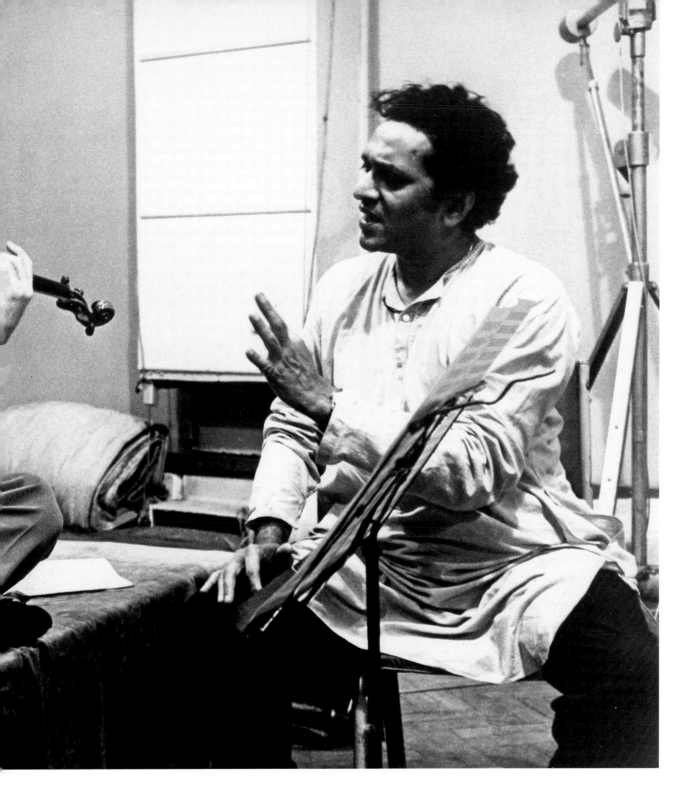

an expressive range fully as large as our own, imbued by that fervent religious dedication which was not so much a religion as a sense of belonging to dimensions and mysteries beyond our comprehension. There are no printed notes in Indian music and one is made aware of the slavery that is imposed on our thoughts and actions by the printed word. The separate intervals and notes are given an importance and discretion they do not have in Western traditions. Everything was sacred in India without being specifically religious—

people were not religious in a church or temple, nor only when they played music, nor was their joy separated from prayer or dedication. It was an extraordinary demonstration of the unity of exuberance, pleasure, abandon, within a form and discipline of the utmost rigor and complexity which in no way inhibited either the sense of reflection or abandon. It was a new breath of life in my own world of music, even while I shared it without participating; for I delayed our association for fifteen years as I felt unequal to it. When I finally took the plunge, it became a renewal of sensation, a rebirth of discovery.

The sessions with Ravi Shankar, a wonderful teacher, were unforgettable and incredibly stimulating. We have made several records and a fine video of our joint performance at the twenty-fifth anniversary of the founding of the United Nations in New York. In our Western musical education only the organist is trained to improvise—as he or she still is in France—and out of that tradition great composers have emerged, as for example César Franck.

*M*y other great experience of improvisation was to play alongside Stéphane Grappelli, a genial human being, almost always in a good mood, who plays his violin without ever practising and is able to improvise on any rhythm or style. When I recorded with him, I noticed he never played the same thing twice—such a thing would be impossible for him! And at each of our sessions he came with a piece of his own composition which we recorded on the spot.

I was thrown into this latter partnership rather unexpectedly when one Christmas morning the BBC in London rang to say that I would be playing with

*S*téphane Grappelli
was the mentor of my second
adventure in the perilous
realm of improvisation.
Even though I was trained,
almost against my nature,
in the classical mode,
the demon of improvisation
has never left me from my earliest
days, and I have always needed
contact with those two masters
of the art, Ravi Shankar
and Stéphane Grappelli, as much
as I needed air to breathe.
Thanks to them, I have been able
to cultivate the love and freshness
of each note played, as if it had
just emerged, newly created
from the depths of my being.
At the moment when he plays,
Stéphane Grappelli must
experience the exhilaration
of being a free man who owes
nothing to anybody
and who depends only
on the inspiration of the moment.
His capacity for improvisation
is such that he is incapable
of playing anything twice
in the same way.
Yehudi Menuhin
and Stéphane Grappelli.

Stéphane Grappelli that night. I was terrified of accepting but desperately wanted to as I can never resist an
adventure. They asked me if I knew any jazz, but the
only melody I knew from my youth was the tango

Jealousy (as a child I had learned to tango, my mother's
idea for me and my sisters). That evening I faced my
first rhythm band and I realized the freedom the
soloist has when the rhythm is covered by someone

*I*n November 1995, Ravi Shankar and I hosted a concert which illustrated in music, dance, and song the history of an epic trek: that of the Gypsies, all the way from Rajasthan to Andalusia. We were able to bring together Indian musicians and dancers, in the sparkling colors of their festive costumes, illustrating various points in their stages north and south of the Mediterranean until we found the synthesis of Gypsy, Arab, Jew, and African in the great flamenco dancer Blanca del Rey, accompanied by the guitarist Manolo San Lucar. All the artists joined in a finale that was led by Ravi Shankar and Blanca del Rey, for they all understood the great nomadic tradition, the tragic and heart-rending experiences of people persecuted along their way, even until today. And they all had the remains of a language in common which enabled them to understand each other—the Gypsies could understand the nomads of Rajasthan, as many of their words were intelligible to each other. This concert was an unforgettable illustration of the eternal interchange between cultures and civilizations, a cross-fertilization of which music is perhaps the greatest example. I liken cultures to gardens in which the flowers and trees send their seed out, borne by the wind, whereas nations I liken to prisons held within their armed frontiers and their prejudices. It is an eternal struggle between the free and the contained, between the improvised and the written, between the rootless and the protected. It is the contrast between a walk on the moon and a walk in one's own garden. Ravi Shankar and Yehudi Menuhin, "From the Sitar to the Guitar," concert. Brussels, November 1995.

else. With the bass or the drum taking care of the tempo, any improvisatory inflection falls into place. In any case it was a great success and the next day French television, who were not able to tolerate the fact that they had been beaten to it by the BBC, demanded a repeat performance. Since then Grappelli and I have made many records and played together on numerous, highly enjoyable occasions.

*M*eeting and talking with musicians such as Ravi Shankar and Stéphane Grappelli has been like a blood transfusion for me. Through them, I discovered something fundamental for the health and practice of classical music. My contact with improvisation enabled me to take another look at our tradition and has colored my way of performing the works of the repertoire. Since these encounters, I have believed that one should study a score with the aim of rediscovering the composer's impulse at the moment when the notes emerged warm and vibrant from the genius of their creator. Music is worth nothing if it is only an act of mechanical repetition. Of course, our work depends on constant practicing, and you cannot perform a piece without playing every molecule of it many, many times. But on the evening of the concert, the composition must appear new and fresh, like those miraculously preserved jewels found in the tombs of the pharaohs. The violinist must try to get as close as possible to this primal emotion of the moment of creation. It seems to me that a cross-fertilization of cultures is the surest way to the most perfect accomplishment of music. The two traditions—improvisation and interpretation—have to intertwine and borrow from each other, for a more intense perfecting of our relationship.

Music, like Joshua's trumpets before the walls of Jericho, can bring even the most indestructible edifices tumbling down. In front of the Berlin Wall, Rostropovich and his cello speak to us of hope and the future. But he is also thinking of the history of events on both sides of the Wall, and he hears the voices of those who sought to escape from the hell inflicted by people on other people. His message reminds us that, beyond the celebration of the moment, there is a longer road to be traveled. Hope never completely abandons the face of the earth, as with this plant, which still proclaims its vital energies despite the disasters of pollution. But hope should never be taken for granted, because then it can too easily transform itself into despair.
Mstislav Rostropovich at the Berlin Wall, 11 November 1989.

*P*ollution on the shores of the Aral Sea, in the former Soviet Union.

EPILOGUE

*M*y instincts have always told me that I was capable of communicating an emotion with the four-stringed instrument that is the violin. In the beginning, when I first became aware of music, this emotion took the form of deep melancholy, and there was nothing I liked better than sad, even tearful, melodies. The song of the Volga boatman, the sobbing tones of the magnificent Russian bass Chaliapin, of whom we had some records at home, and the languorous, mournful airs of Russian, Jewish, and Gypsy violinists—all plunged me into a state of complete rapture. Fortunately, I was also listening to the classical repertoire as played by the San

Francisco Symphony Orchestra: in those days the only recordings available were of three to four minutes duration. My mother adored Russian folk music, and when she was in a good mood she would dance to a tune or two; and I would often hear my father singing the Hasidic melodies of his childhood. Thus the world of my tastes and aspirations began to expand.

The spark was lit when I was seven years old, on a pavement in San Francisco at the artists' entrance to the Curran Theater, where I had already once seen Anna Pavlova dance. I succumbed ineluctably to the charm of this beautiful creature, but on that particular day it was her luggage which fired my imagination. The sight of those six or seven trunks, presumably filled with her costumes and those of her company, this luggage all neatly arranged along the pavement and waiting to be carried off somewhere to the other side of the world, had a tremendous effect on me. It seemed to me that the trunks contained within their closed confines a thousand and one voyages, and that the most brilliant spectacles, the most romantic adventures, had left their memories in them. I felt that by looking at them a bit of the magic of touring would rub off on me.

I was like the character in the Pirandello short story, *The Train Whistle Blew*, a modest man who lived a poor life in a drab, ugly building. Every evening at the same time he would hear the whistle of a train passing his window, and he began to dream of voyages. The simple whistle of that train conjured up fantasies of discovery and adventure that he had never experienced and probably never would.

Just like him, as I looked at Pavlova's luggage, I dreamed of what I was going to achieve with the violin. Without being consciously aware of it, I was imagining all kinds of things that might enable me to go beyond ordinary life. I constructed a thousand plans to transcend the everyday. As an innocent pyromaniac, an unconscious arsonist, I had set fire to life and lit the flame which has guided me from that day to this. The fiery Russian part of my mother, and the social and humanitarian part of my father, who always dedicated himself in compassion for others, served as fuel for this furnace.

I have been able to realize this dream in two ways: first, by becoming a violinist, which has allowed me to travel the world, just as I had promised myself; and then, one lunchtime in 1944, in meeting the woman who was to become my wife. I found her sitting on a footstool at her mother's house. Diana Gould, the daughter of a famous pianist and a diplomat, was the most beautiful dancer I had spent my life looking for. At the time of our meeting she was acting with Michael Redgrave in a play by Hugo Werfel, *Jakobsky and the Colonel*. I saw in Diana a kind of reincarnation of Pavlova, a mirror image of her beauty and romanticism. She fired my being in the same way that Pavlova had fired my childhood imaginings, and she continues to this day.

*M*usic and, more particularly, the violin are for me threads that weave hearts and minds together, not only in symbolic ways, but in ways that are very real and concrete. Music, and art in general, are not optional extras. One cannot think of them as useless accessories to humanity: dance, song, and other forms of expression have always been there to celebrate life's rituals, and the joys and values of living. The composers, painters, and poets of yesterday and today show us that art, so far from being an escape from reality, actually enables us to approach reality along a pure and direct path. Since the beginning of history, artists have tried to say that art was in fact more intense, more real than life, so that others, receiving a small part of their love and devotion, might cease hating and fighting.

I will never forget what I was once told by Rebecca Godchaux, the dear French lady who gave me my first lessons in that most poetical language, when I was nine years old in San Francisco: "My dear," she said, "as long as there are men, there will be war." Such a statement was a terrible shock for me. In the world as I knew it then, it was impossible for me to share her resignation; the idea was appalling, and I have never ceased to fight against it. It seemed to me that with the violin I could act as a counterweight to that inexorable evil. I thought that I could bring peace to the world through and with music.

I realized as the years passed that I was a bit naive, and that my actions could not possibly have such powerful, beneficial effects: Rebecca may well have been right. Yet I have never lost the idealism of my youth; I firmly believe that music can bring people together and heal them, and I have single-mindedly pursued my youthful determination, doing as much as I could with the means that were available to me. I am convinced that music—because it keeps us in contact with the world, because it helps us see ourselves as part of the vibrant cosmos—shapes the conscious and the unconscious in us, and creates a harmony within each of us and with each other.

The work I do in my Foundation—the various projects that have been set up over the years—and

in my schools, proceed from this unshakable faith in the salutary power for humanity of singing, dancing, and art. This work may eventually culminate, I pray, in a European Parliament of Cultures, to become a counterweight to the parliament of states. Perhaps one day the artist that slumbers in every one of us will find a response to political parties. Perhaps one day the human instincts of domination will find other channels of expression—not in fighting and aggression, but in music, sculpture, theater, sport, adventure, and the pursuit of knowledge and discovery. Perhaps one day, under the beneficent influence of artistic activity, the hypocrisy and schizophrenia which give us such easy alibis for not seeing the misery around us, for not taking action in Sarajevo and elsewhere, will become a thing of the past, in the same way as human science has succeeded in eradicating certain illnesses.

If I had to define more specifically how the violin can contribute to the beneficial role of music, I would say two things. First, the violin as an instrument teaches us a lot about relations between people and the world. Playing the violin demands a suppleness, an openness, and a flexibility which, if they were applied to human relations, would radically change the course of history: with the violin, the spirit of possession, the urge to dominate, and aggression have no place. The violin and its bow have to be held with infinite tenderness and great delicacy. The violin teaches the person who plays it basic qualities that are fundamentally salutary for society.

I would also say that the voice of the violin, this melody that nothing can interrupt, not even breathing (here violinists have the edge on singers, in the sense that they do not have to stop their playing to take a breath—although they often should when they do not)—this melody expresses an unbroken pulse within society, a heart that beats, the purity of a line. We live in a fragmented world surrounded by meaningless noises, hemmed in by rhythms produced by the banging, scratching, and clicking of machines and all kinds of electrical gadgetry. All that this gives us is fatigue and irritability, and were it not for the tireless course of the sun that rises every morning and sets every evening, it would sometimes be hard to maintain any kind of contact with nature, emotion, and life.

This is why the violin, through the serene clarity of its song, helps us keep our bearings in the storm: as a light in the night, a compass in the tempest, it shows us the way to a haven of sincerity and respect. In the violin, there is an honesty of purpose: you cannot cheat, you cannot betray. The violin spurs one to musical acts of devotion: Georges Enesco and Ravi Shankar, those two priests of music who conceived their art as an offering, as a rite, inculcated that same respect in me. With them and thanks to them, I have a sense of living my music, of bringing it to life, in the same way that I would light incense tapers.

It has taken us centuries to elaborate our musical scales and perfect our instruments. The sensibilities, the genius, and the hearts of many people have worked to create this heritage from within which we can, every day and without end, draw a little light and emotion. Music therefore has to be played with devotion. Its power and its history should breathe solemnity, nobility, and a sense of the sacred into the person who plays its notes, and into the listener. Through its diaphanous voice, the violin expresses the desire for purity that vibrates in the hearts of all people. It enables us to rediscover the secret path by which things can come together, within us and among us.

CONTENTS

PICTURE CREDITS

ADAGP, Paris, 1996/Artephot: 6 (photo A. Held, Hulton Collection, London), 197 (photo Martin, private collection, Switzerland)

ADAGP, Paris, 1996/Dagli Orti: 52–53 (Saint Paul-de-Vence, Fondation A. Maeght), 252–53 (private collection, Switzerland)

ADAGP, Paris, 1996/Magnum: 101 (photo Erich Lessing, Kunstsammlung-Nordrhein-Westphalen, Düsseldorf)

Agence VU, 30–31 (photo Larry Fink), 107 (photo Tono Stano), 108–9 (photo Gérard Rondeau), 118 (photo Graziela Iturbide), 122–3 (photo Gérard Rondeau), 126–7 (photo Larry Fink), 180–1 (photo Anthony Suau), 284–5 (photo Graziela Iturbide)

Alain-Michel Sobotik, 124, 124–5, 290

EMI Archives, 286–7 (photo David Farrell), 289 (photo Peter Vernon)

Archive Photos, 94–5, 170–1, 213 top, 213 bottom (photo G. D. Hackett), 216–17, 226–7, 232–3

Artephot, 6 (photo A. Held, Hulton Collection, London), 34–5 (photo Nimatallah, Museen Preussischer Kulturbesitz, Berlin–Dahlem), 166 (photo Nimatallah, Galleria dell'Academia, Venice), 197 (photo Martin, private collection, Switzerland)

Artothek, 57 (Städelsches Kunstinstitut, Frankfurt)

Bildarchiv Preussischer Kulturbesitz, 71 (photo Hanns Hubmann), 88–9, 111 (photo Liepe), 128, 136, 151 (photo E. Bieber), 153, 154–5 (photo P. Loescher and Petsch), 172, 204, 218–9 (National Portrait Gallery, London), 220 (Galerie Tretjakov, Moscow), 223 (Sibelius Museum, Turku, Finland), 239 (photo Siegfried Lauterwasser), 249

Bridgeman Art Library, 188–9 (Gavin Graham Gallery, London)

Cosmos, 258–9 (photo Brian Vikander)

Dagli Orti, 10 (Musée du Louvre, Paris), 17 (National Library, Rio de Janeiro), 20–21 (Museo del Prado, Madrid), 22 (National Museum of Archaeology, Athens), 32 (National Library,

Naples), 47 (National Museum, Tokyo), 52–3 (Fondation A. Maeght, Saint Paul-de-Vence), 64 (Notre-Dame Cathedral, Reims), 67 (Musée Correr, Venice), 68–9 (private collection), 70 (Prado, Madrid), 76 (Navarre Museum, Pamplona), 77 (Château de Gien, Musée international de la Chasse), 99 (Museo Soares dos Reis, Porto) 104–5 (Musée d'Art colonial de Santa Catalina, Cuzco, Peru), 110 (Musée Granet, Aix-en-Provence), 112–13 (Musée de la Ville, Vienna), 129 (Société des Amis de la musique, Vienna), 137 (Greig's House, Bergen, Norway), 146 (Musée archéologique, Naples), 187 (Bach Archives, Leipzig), 191 (Bibliothèque Marciana, Venice), 194–5 (Bibliothèque Marciana, Venice) 198 (Conservatoire de Musique de San Pietro, Naples), 203 (Galerie d'Art moderne, Florence), 210–11 (Bela Bartók's House, Budapest, Hungary), 224 (Musée Granet, Aix-en-Provence), 228–9 (Institute of Arts, Detroit), 246–7 (Musée de la Ville, Vienna), 251 (Prado, Madrid), 252–3 (private collection, Switzerland), 260–1 (Musée du Louvre, Paris)

DEMART PRO ARTE B.V./ADAGP 1996/Artephot: 197 (photo Martin, private collection, Switzerland)

© DR: 135, 140–1 (EMI Archives), 142 (EMI Archives)

Enguerand, 60–1 (photo Agostino Pacciani), 200–1 (photo Colette Masso, 206–7 (photo Sophie Steinberger)

Explorer, 80–1 (photo J. Delaborde), 273 (photo J. L. S. Dubois), 274 (photo J. M. Steinlein), 276–7 (photo A. Reffet, Sakya monastery, Lhagon, Tibet, Kham [Sichuan])

Flammarion, 164–5 (photo Frédéric Morellec)

François Canard, 266–7

Guy Vivien, 90–1

Jacques Six, 256–7

Jean Galodé, 41

Magnum, 11 (photo Erich Lessing, Musée du Louvre, Paris), 18–19 (photo Erich Lessing, Uffizi, Florence), 26 (photo Werner Bischof), 27 (photo Werner Bischof), 42 (photo Dennis Stock), 43 (photo Marc Riboud), 48 (photo René Burri), 50–1 (photo Michael K. Nichols), 54–5 (photo Stuart Franklin), 58–9 (photo Marilyn Silverstone), 73 (photo Erich Lessing, Musée du Louvre, Paris), 86–7 (photo T. Hoepker, Metropolitan Museum of Arts, New York), 98 (photo Erich Lessing, Musée des Beaux-Arts, Lille), 101 (photo Erich Lessing, Kunstsammlung-Nordrhein-Westfalen, Düsseldorf), 114–15 (photo Erich Lessing, Palais de Schönbrunn, Vienne), 117 (photo Erich Lessing, Haydn Museum, Rohrau, Austria), 120–1 (photo Josef Koudelka), 131 (photo Eve Arnold), 144–5 (photo S. Franklin), 149 (photo Erich Lessing, Mozart's House, Salzburg); 156–7 (photo Martine Franck), 160–1 (photo Martine Franck), 163 (photo Eve Arnold), 169 (photo Inge Morath), 186 (photo Erich Lessing, Haydn Museum, Eidenstadt, Austria), 192 (photo Erich Lessing, Museum der Bildenden Künste, Leipzig), 221 (photo Inge Morath), 236 (photo Eugene W. Smith), 240–1 (photo Erich Hartmann), 242–3 (photo Erich Lessing, Oesterreichische Galerie,

Vienna), 245 (photo Marilyn Silverstone), 254–5 (photo Fred Mayer), 280–1 (photo Henri Cartier-Bresson), 282–3 (photo Josef Koudelka), 293 (photo Fred Mayer)

Musée de l'Homme, 14 (photo M. Griaule), 265 (photo M. Delaplanche), 268 (photo M. Dela-planche), 269 (photo C. Lemazaouda), 272 (photo G. Rouget), 275 (photo J. Oster and D. Destable)

M. Horvath/Anzenberger/Cosmos, 83, 92–3

Photothèque des musées de la Ville de Paris, 250 (photo Pierrain), Musée du Petit Palais, Paris)

Rapho, 44–5 (photo Roland and Sabrina Michaud), 271 (photo Roland and Sabrina Michaud)

RMN, 37 (Musée du Louvre, Paris), 147 (Cabinet des dessins, Musée du Louvre, Paris)

Robert Bégouën, 12, 13

Roger-Viollet, 38–9 (photo Lipnitzki-Viollet), 62, 84–5 (Bibliothèque nationale, Paris), 97, 134, 139, 150, 175, 176–7, 178, 183, 184–5 (photo Harlingue-Viollet), 225 (Palais Querini, Venice), 230, 234–5 (photo Lipnitzki-Viollet)

Royal College of Music, 215

Scala, 74–5 (Galerie Palatina, Florence), 78–9 (Santuario, Saronno, Italy), 102 (Museo Teatrale alla Scala, Milan), 199 (Museo Bibliografico Musicale, Bologna)

SPADEM 1996/Dagli Orti: 52–3 (Fondation A. Maeght, Saint Paul-de-Vence)

SPADEM 1996/Bildarchiv Preussischer Kulturbesitz: 250 (Galerie Tretjakov, Moscow)

Stars and Stripes/Sygma, 292

Sygma, 25 (photo Eric Robert), 158–9 (photo Haruyosih Yamaguchi, 264 (photo F. Soltan)

Times Newspapers Limited, 262–3 (photo Michael Powell)

With the exception of the photographs credited above, several works in this book belong to the personal collection of Lord Yehudi Menuhin and are reproduced with his kind permission: pages: 7, 9, 138, 209, 278.

The picture on pages 132–3 belongs to the personal collection of B. K. S. Iyengar (RIMYI Archives, Poona, India).

The picture on page 279 belongs to the personal collection of Dr. A. Subramanian.

© 1996 ADAGP for the works by Pierre Bonnard, Marc Chagall, Salvador Dalí, Paul Klee.
© 1996 SPADEM for the works by Pierre Bonnard, Iosif A. Serebrjanyj.
© 1996 D.R. for the works by Kenneth Green, Max Oppenheimer, Teodor Schalin.

4294021